Video in Language Teaching

NEW DIRECTIONS IN LANGUAGE TEACHING
Editors: Howard B. Altman and Peter Strevens

This important new series is for language teachers and others who:
– need to be informed about the key issues facing the language teaching profession today;
– want to understand the theoretical issues underlying current debates;
– wish to relate theory to classroom practice.

In this series:
Communicative Language Teaching: an introduction by William Littlewood
Developing Reading Skills: a practical guide to reading comprehension exercises by Françoise Grellet
Simulations in Language Teaching by Ken Jones
Video in Language Teaching by Jack Lonergan

Video in Language Teaching

Jack Lonergan

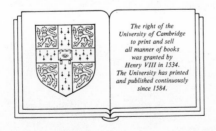

The right of the
University of Cambridge
to print and sell
all manner of books
was granted by
Henry VIII in 1534.
The University has printed
and published continuously
since 1584.

Cambridge University Press
Cambridge
London   New York   New Rochelle
Melbourne   Sydney

Published by the Press Syndicate of the University of Cambridge
The Pitt Building, Trumpington Street, Cambridge CB2 1RP
32 East 57th Street, New York, NY 10022, USA
296 Beaconsfield Parade, Middle Park, Melbourne 3206, Australia

© Cambridge University Press 1984

First published 1984

Printed in Great Britain at The Pitman Press, Bath

Library of Congress catalogue card number: 83-20869

British Library cataloguing in publication data

Lonergan, Jack

Video in language teaching. – (New
directions in language teaching)
1. Languages, Modern – Study and teaching
– Audio-visual aids
2. Video tape recorders and recordings
I. Title   II. Series
418'.007'8   PB36

ISBN 0 521 25270 9 hard covers
ISBN 0 521 27263 7 paperback

Contents

Thanks

My close involvement with multi-media language teaching began in the fortunate context of running the federal teacher-training scheme set up to introduce *Follow Me* into adult education institutions in West Germany. I owe a great deal to the many teachers and teacher trainers who worked on that project, and particularly to Tony Fitzpatrick, Deutscher Volkshochschul-Verband; Heinz Gaderer, Verband Oesterreichischer Volkshochschulen; and Brian Hill, Brighton Polytechnic. Both then and subsequently, the co-operation and support of producers and publishers of language-teaching television and video materials have been crucial to the development of ideas, and I express my thanks to the following and their colleagues: Beatriz Casoy, Evans Bros.; Michael Cass, Longman Group; Peter Collier, Cornelsen and Oxford University Press; Doug Davidson, Nelson Filmscan; Bruce Duncan-Smith, Formavision, Paris; Chris Faram, BBC English by Radio; Hugh Howse, BBC English by Radio and Television; Mary Law, Thames Television; John McGovern, British Council; Jean-Michel Ploton, Armand-Colin / Longman; Gerhard Vogel, Norddeutscher Rundfunk; Horst Weise, Bayerischer Rundfunk.

Detailed advice on this manuscript has been gratefully accepted from Peter Donovan at Cambridge University Press. The hectic manuscript preparation was dealt with by Valerie Davidson, whom I thank gratefully. The calm and constancy of home life which provides an environment for writing a book is supplied by my wife, whom I cannot thank enough.

Jack Lonergan
London 1983

A note on copying video material

The copying and off-air recording of broadcast and published video material is usually illegal if unauthorised. The techniques for using video in language teaching described in this book apply strictly to authorised use of video material. Those intending to use such material should ensure that permission to record or duplicate material is obtained from the copyright holder. In some cases, educational use of off-air recording may be allowed within specified limitations. However, it is the responsibility of the user to ensure that permission to copy broadcast or published video material exists before any such copies are made.

Introduction

The purpose of this book

Video in the classroom offers exciting possibilities for language teaching and learning. This book is intended to be a practical guide to the use of video in the language classroom. The principles of effective teaching and learning are illustrated with examples from a wide range of material, at all levels of language learning.

Most of the examples are taken from English language teaching; the examples from French and German demonstrate that the principles are applicable to any language. Consequently, this book is intended for teachers and teacher trainers concerned with the teaching of any foreign language. The methodological implications of using video in class mean that this book can also benefit course designers, materials writers, and producers and publishers of language-teaching materials on video tape.

The term 'video' is often used to mean quite different things in language teaching. For some, it means no more than replaying television programmes on a video recorder, for viewing in class or private study. For others, it implies the use of a video camera in class to record and play back to learners their activities and achievements in a foreign language. These and many other uses of video equipment are discussed fully in this book. The distinctions between the various activities are, of course, made clear.

This book is not intended as a technical guide to the range of equipment that new technology is making available to language teachers. Nor can it be concerned in detail with the specifications and performance of equipment now on the market or being developed. However, a brief guide to how video equipment works is included in chapter 10. Throughout the book there are references to technical facilities on video equipment and how they can be used effectively in the language classroom.

The aim of most language learning is to acquire the ability to communicate with others in the target language. The process of language teaching and learning should also be communicative. The examples in this book assume a communicative approach to language teaching. But the theme is the classroom use of video equipment. This means that the descriptions of the various ways in which the equipment can be used in class must influence the structure of the book. The chapters are presented in a sequence which can serve as a guided introduction to the use of video for those with little previous experience. Others will be able to draw on any relevant part of the book, as appropriate to their specific needs in their own particular language teaching and learning situations.

Background to the book

Language-teaching programmes form a significant part of educational broadcasting, especially in Western Europe. Radio and television have made important contributions to foreign language learning.

The widespread use of video recorders has had two main effects on language-teaching broadcasts. The first of these is to free teaching institutions and learners from the constraints of the broadcasting timetable. Video recorders can be used to store programmes for showing at any convenient time. The second change concerns how television programmes are made. Appreciating the benefits that a video recorder brings into the classroom, more producers of language-teaching materials are designing video tape materials with the classroom exploitation in mind. Four or five minutes of video tape material can easily provide enough stimulating input for one hour's teaching. There has consequently been a move away from twenty-minute or half-hour programmes, towards programmes which can be conveniently subdivided into sections of only a few minutes length. A central theme in this book is how to maximise those few minutes in terms of language-learning potential.

Organisation of the book

Each chapter and subsection deals with one particular aspect of teaching with video, as the headings indicate. This is intended to be helpful in a practical guide to the use of video in the classroom, though it means that topics are treated in isolation. Where practical, cross-references are made to other aspects of language teaching. Throughout, topics are illustrated with extracts from language-teaching courses, and the teacher is invited to transfer principles illustrated in one section of the book to other examples in the book or to the local language-teaching situation.

Chapter 1 introduces video films as a language-teaching aid. Teaching with a video can be exciting, but it is not a new methodology. The main principles of good language teaching can be applied to video equipment, which remains nevertheless an additional resource.

Although video presentations are stimulating, and generally capture the interest of viewers, it is disheartening for language learners to be unable to follow a sequence because of language difficulties. In chapter 2 several suggestions are made for helping language learners to follow video sequences. Chapter 3 shows how the transition from viewing and comprehension to active production can be made. At this stage in the language-learning process, the material on the video is likely to be treated as a model, to be imitated in some degree by the learners.

In chapter 4 attention is drawn to the wealth of visual information that is presented on video. Aspects of communication such as gestures and facial expressions are exploited for a variety of language-learning activities. Consideration is also given to the way language functions in specific communicative situations.

Television and video are powerful media which apparently offer little chance for interaction between screen and viewer. Some of the suggestions made in the book attempt to overcome this. In chapter 5 a detailed account is given of how language-learning activities can develop from the media input. It is important that language learners recognise how the communicative content of video presentations can be related to their own language-learning needs.

The soundtrack of video tapes carries an important part of the communicative message. In chapter 6 there are various suggestions for developing language activities based on the soundtrack.

The assumption is made in most of the book that language teachers using video will have access to appropriate language-teaching materials. It is clear that in many teaching institutions these are not available; or that other materials are needed to supplement them. Subject to local copyright restrictions, recordings can be made of television broadcasts, and these can be used for stimulating language work. Several approaches to the use of off-air recordings are given in chapter 7. Professional broadcasts bring a level of expertise and excellence into the classroom that language teachers can never match. Nevertheless, it is exciting and stimulating to work with a video camera with language learners. Chapter 8 offers a simple introduction to operating a video camera; the assumption is made that the teacher has the minimum equipment: one video camera only. Further suggestions for making video recordings with learners are given in chapter 9. Chapter 10 offers a beginner's introduction to video equipment.

Some topics have been deliberately excluded from this book. For example, the interesting experiment in offering a language test on national television to the population as a whole (carried out in West Germany in connection with the *Follow Me* project in 1980) has been ignored. Similarly, the fascinating possibilities of high-quality information retrieval offered by video discs are also excluded. However, the book will succeed if it makes teachers and teacher trainers aware of the existing possibilities for using video equipment in the classroom, and encourages them to make the most of this valuable resource.

1   Video films as a language-teaching aid

1.1   The communicative value of video films

The outstanding feature of video films is their ability to present complete communicative situations. The combination of sound and vision is dynamic, immediate, and accessible. This means that communication can be shown in a context, and the many factors in communication can be perceived easily by viewers – and language learners.

The speakers in dialogues can be seen and heard; other participants in the situation can be seen. The language learner can readily see the ages of the participants; their sex; perhaps their relationships one to another; their dress, social status, and what they are doing; and perhaps their mood or feelings. Further, paralinguistic information, such as facial expressions or hand gestures, is available to accompany aural clues of intonation.

Similarly, the setting of the communication is clear: the language learner can see on the screen where the action is taking place. This information may help to clarify whether the situation is very formal, or perhaps informal.

Of course, these audio-visual features of video films are found in cinema films and television broadcasts too. But these other media do not offer the same facilities for classroom exploitation of the material and content that video recorders do. How to make the best use of the rich resources of video recordings forms the main part of this book.

A further feature of video recordings – which is shared with other related media – is the use of electronic tricks to create special effects and images. These are usually quite beyond the resources of the language teacher to produce, and provide another valuable source of material for use in language teaching and learning.

1.2   The power of the medium

The power of television as a medium is acknowledged by all, even if its benefits and disadvantages are a matter for controversy. Video films in language teaching have advantages and drawbacks which spring from the power of television as a medium. At their best, video presentations will be intrinsically interesting to language learners. The learner will want to watch, even if comprehension is limited. The material should be motivating; the learner should want to see more, to ask questions, to follow up ideas and suggestions. By generating interest and motivation, the video films can create a climate for successful learning. However, most learners are used to watching television screens in a domestic context: feature films, plays, quizzes, variety shows, news and sports programmes are the staple diet of television broadcasts. The vast majority of viewers watch for relaxation and entertainment; they are pleased that the television has so much to offer. They are also pleased that the television makes no demands on them; the output of the television is available to all at the end of a working day, for example – and there is no need to take any special action. In a language-learning context, there is a need for special action: inter-action with the video.

1.3 The role of the teacher

As in most language-teaching situations, the role of the teacher is a key one. It is the teacher who must harness the power of the video films; it is the teacher who has the prime responsibility for creating a successful learning environment.

Video is another useful aid for the language teacher. It is not meant to rival or overshadow the teacher, still less replace her or him. By the skilful use of the various techniques that modern technology makes available, language teachers can choose to present video materials to learners in the most suitable way for facilitating successful language acquisition. In this, teachers should be helped by support materials supplied with the video films, or which they devise for themselves. Many video films incorporate sequences specially designed for classroom use. Some examples of this are given in later chapters.

If a video camera is used in class, the responsibility for the video film, and how it is used, will also lie with the teacher – certainly in the early stages with any particular class. In a later chapter, we discuss how learners can co-operate in producing video material, and some considerations for the teacher when playing self-made materials to the learners.

The successful use of any teaching aid – printed materials, blackboards, flashcards, overhead projectors, and so on – presupposes the successful application of certain pedagogical principles to teaching. This applies to the use of video in class too, and is the main concern of the various chapters of this book. Yet for many teachers, working with video recorders and cameras is a new experience. As such, technical considerations and problems can dominate the activity. Teachers might not be sure which cable is which, which button performs which function; there may be embarrassment all round if there is a technical fault which the teacher cannot repair. This insecurity can lead teachers to doing nothing else with video films than switching them on, letting the class watch them, and then turning them off. The rest of the lesson then proceeds as though there has been no use of the video at all.

It is clear that teachers must be confident and competent when handling the video equipment: chapter 10 offers an absolute beginner's guide to the controls on a video recorder. The examples given in the following chapters include some which are specifically designed to introduce teachers to working with video equipment – recorders and cameras. However, the responsibility for successful language learning does not rest with the teacher alone; she or he might create the right conditions for language learning, but the learners must respond to the situation.

1.4 The role of the learner

Watching video films for language-learning purposes should be an active process by the learners. Yet most language learners will be experienced in passive television viewing as domestic viewing tends to be passive. The support materials made by the teacher or supplied with the films should encourage positive viewing by the learners; they must participate so that the output from the video is not just one-way, to an unresponsive audience. Techniques for promoting active viewing are given in the next chapter; and in later chapters there is discussion of ways in which this active viewing can be transferred to group-work activities among the learners.

Many learners have difficulty relating to video as a valuable teaching aid. Domestic television has such strong connotations of entertainment that the expectation of many learners, when watching video language-teaching material, is that they are to be entertained. Although there is a need for language-teaching materials to be entertaining, the nature of the entertainment is of course quite different. It is essential, therefore, that learners are introduced gradually to video in the classroom, and guided to an understanding of how valuable the medium can be.

If learners are to be recorded on video tape, with a camera in the class, this point is equally relevant. It may take some time for initial feelings of amusement, embarrassment or insecurity to die down. The first shock of seeing the complete self-image on screen is often greater than hearing one's own voice recorded on audio tape for the first time.

But when learners are at ease with the video equipment, and appreciate the positive benefits for language learning when it is used constructively, the way is open to a wide variety of learner-centred activities.

With recorded video materials, learners can take responsibility for choosing sequences for review; learners can stop films when they are interesting, and ask their own questions about what is presented. Used in the library mode, providing self-access or private-study facilities for learners, the same materials can be a stimulating source of language material which the learner can control.

If a video camera is available, then the learners can take over the role of producer. Rather than the teacher merely recording what the learners say or do, the learners themselves set up projects – in the target language. This may involve scripting, speaking, interviewing, reporting – in fact, a wide range of interesting, highly motivating activities that a learner can identify with.

In short: the role of the learner is to be a creative member in a joint partnership – the video equipment, the teacher, and the learner.

1.5 The variety of video materials

Video materials used in language teaching can come from a wide variety of sources. The techniques for using the video in class outlined in the following chapters can be used, as appropriate, with different sorts of films, whether they were designed for language-teaching purposes or not. We can categorise the sources of video films broadly as follows:
– video recordings of language-teaching broadcasts and films;
– video recordings of domestic television broadcasts, such as comedy programmes and news programmes;
– video recordings of specialist films and television programmes, such as documentaries produced by industry, or educational programmes;
– video language-teaching materials made for the classroom rather than for public transmission as broadcasts;
– self-made video films, involving the teachers and learners.

The term 'video film' is used rather loosely. Film is a photographic process, involving the effects of light and chemicals on sensitive paper. Holiday snapshots and cinema films are made on photographic film. Recording on video tape is an electronic process, using magnetic tape. Audio cassette and video camera recordings are made on magnetic tape. The material shown on domestic television is drawn from both sources, but broadcast electronically. Any recordings of broadcasts made on a video recorder are also on video (magnetic) tape. When played back on the television screen, these video materials look like small screen films – and so the inaccurate term 'video films'.

Video recordings of language-teaching broadcasts and films

Films made for language teaching have the obvious merit of being planned and produced for a language-learning audience. This means that the language may be graded, and that the presentation of new vocabulary items, structures, or speech exponents will be controlled. The film is likely to have an explicit language-learning goal, expressed in terms of language structures or a level of communicative ability; and if not, accompanying written materials might be available to guide classroom discussions of what is presented on film. The language used and the situations shown are likely to relate well to other published materials, such as study guides and course books, or to recognised syllabuses or examinations.

These and other features of films made for broadcast are attractive to both teachers and learners. Nonetheless, broadcasts have disadvantages, too, which are still evident when the films are shown on video. The video recording offers the facility of seeing the original broadcast many times over, and so the problem of the ephemerality of broadcasts is overcome. But broadcasts – and films – are designed to be seen in one sitting, with no interruptions, no replays, no slow motion. The following chapters demonstrate how important it is that a selection should be made from films when they are shown on video equipment in class; how the facilities of the video recorder should be exploited to gain the maximum benefit from the films.

Video recordings of domestic television broadcasts

These materials, which have not been produced for language-teaching purposes, can be used in the classroom to bring to language learning the same benefits as the use of other realia, such as newspaper articles, magazine pictures, or popular records. They are real and meaningful; and they have a relevance to the learner which transcends the immediate needs of language learning.

There are occasions when it is quite legitimate just to play a recording of a broadcast, using the video recorder to show television programmes at a time convenient for the learners. For example, during an intensive residential course many learners might welcome the chance to relax for the evening in front of an adventure movie in the target language. But, generally speaking, such material needs preparation and follow-up work, and presentation to the learner in shorter sequences than the whole film. The use of the word 'legitimate' above refers of course to pedagogical considerations, rather than legal aspects of using recordings of television broadcasts. Many feature films and documentaries are available for sale or hire in video cassette form. It is important to remember that in many countries, recording material off-air from broadcasts, or re-copying recordings, infringes copyright and is illegal.

Video recordings of specialist films and television programmes

Many industries and individual companies produce films to inform the general public and specialists about aspects of their work. These films, which may have their roots in public relations as well as education, are usually readily available on video cassette, often with fewer copyright restrictions than ordinary television broadcasts. Similarly, programmes made for the educational channels of broadcasting authorities are usually available to the public, with few copyright problems affecting their use in language-teaching institutions.

The thematic content of many of these films means that they are particularly suitable for courses in language for specific purposes; some suggestions for using these films are given below. A possible problem, unless the learners are advanced, is the level of language used in specialist films. For many teachers of, say, French in non-Francophone countries, such films are not available anyway. In this case, films recorded in the native language can still be adapted for, say, French language-training purposes: the original soundtrack is ignored, and the visual information is used for language work.

Video language materials made for the classroom

Video materials made for the classroom (or self-study unit) can have all the advantages that the medium of television brings, as well as being designed specially for the purpose of educational use. Just as it is standard practice to make audio cassette materials in a way different from radio broadcasts, so these video films are quite different in construction from the usual television language broadcasts. In the broadcast mode, television programmes are presented in a linear fashion: the programme starts, and progresses without pauses or review to the end. The viewer cannot stop, consider, or look again at an earlier passage – as a reader can with this book, for example. Language programmes made specifically for video take into account the fact that the video recorder does allow for selective viewing, which breaks into linear progression of the programme. And television broadcasts, once on video tape, can be treated in the same way as the video programmes (see chapter 7).

The developments in technology and the spread of video equipment into homes, offices and educational institutions all indicate that these types of language-learning materials will become increasingly popular, both for classroom work, and self-study.

Self-made video films

Working with a video camera can be very exciting, both for the teacher and the learners. However, there are so many apparent pitfalls that many teachers doubt their competence to handle a camera in the language classroom. A structured guide to the first stages of using a camera is given in chapter 8. Many of the considerations mentioned above, concerning the use of video films in the classroom, also apply to self-made films. The major difference, of course, lies in the fact that the subject of these films is usually the learners themselves. The film can be used to analyse their use of language, their gestures and their reactions, as well as to provide a record of activities and plays which might be performed.

The camera can also be used to record things outside the classroom: silent movies can be made, or mystery films, for example, to encourage speculation and discussion among the learners. As indicated earlier in this chapter, the learners can also be given charge of the camera to develop their own video projects in the target language (see chapter 9).

1.6   A valuable resource

This chapter has highlighted some of the key issues to be borne in mind when considering the use of video for language teaching and learning. The remaining chapters consider these and other issues in more detail; and provide examples of the application of some of the principles mentioned to practical classroom situations.

Foreign-language acquisition is a complicated process; a few isolated illustrations, such as in this book, cannot encompass the many different aspects of language learning, nor the many different language-teaching situations. The examples given are therefore intended to be illustrative; the reader should be able to transfer the underlying principles to the local situation and to the materials at hand.

In closing this chapter, it should be stressed that the use of video in language teaching does not entail a completely new language-teaching methodology. The best principles of using other teaching aids and resources should be applied critically to the possible uses of video equipment. It may well be that the special nature of video films, with their powerful communicative content, influences the style of teachers and learners. The following chapters are intended as a guide to the successful use of a most valuable resource in language teaching and learning.

A large number of language-teaching video programmes are referred to in the text. Each reference is made by title only; details of the programmes are all listed separately in Bibliography A: Materials referred to in the text.

2 Active viewing and comprehension

2.1 Introduction

We have seen that it is necessary for language learners to take an active part in viewing video materials. This chapter shows how active viewing can focus the learners' attention on certain parts of the video presentation; this focus is intended, of course, to benefit the language-learning capabilities of the learners. At the same time, active viewing can increase the enjoyment and satisfaction gained from viewing, as well as maintain the learners' motivation.

The comprehension of video sequences by learners is complex, and varies between individuals. As well as the language structures and lexical items used in a communicative situation there are the paralinguistic cues; in the background is a wealth of non-linguistic information. No learner can realistically demonstrate the extent to which *all* the information received has been understood; it is rarely desirable that learners should even attempt such a comprehensive task. For this reason, the viewing guides illustrated in the following sections, which are used to encourage active viewing, are not intended to test comprehension. Viewing guides are intended to aid comprehension. It is essential that the contents of the guides are known or taught before learners watch the video sequence.

Because a video presentation shows the totality of a communicative situation, it is usually difficult for learners to undertake extensive writing – or reading – tasks while watching the screen. Viewing guides which are to be completed simultaneously with viewing the video sequence should therefore be so constructed that the reading and writing load for the learner is kept to a minimum; the reading is usually necessary for the learner to know what to do, or how far he or she has progressed; the writing is the active demonstration of comprehension.

However, the techniques of stopping and starting video tapes, which are discussed more fully in later chapters, mean that learners can write notes or opinions about sections of video presentations as the film progresses. In each case, a writing pause, or even a review of the video material, is built into the whole presentation of the video material. This applies not only to the classroom use of video records, but also to private study, if facilities are available for individuals or groups to have access to video materials in a library or self-study centre.

2.2 Guided selection

In the examples in this section, language output from the learner is kept to a minimum. Comprehension is shown by marking the prepared viewing guide with just a cross or tick. The task is made very easy, as the learner only has to choose from a limited number of options, one of which is known to be correct. The examples are taken from the *Media Teaching Manual* prepared for *Follow Me*, unit 4 – that is, suitable for a class of adult beginners after four weeks of part-time study (say two to three hours per week). The thematic and functional area is location and direction: asking for and giving information. The first example focuses on direction:

VIEWING GUIDE

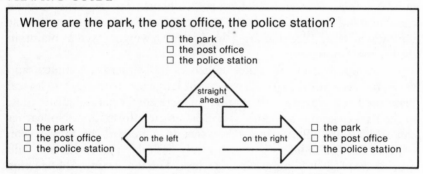

Where are the park, the post office, the police station?

☐ the park
☐ the post office
☐ the police station

straight ahead

☐ the park   on the left   on the right   ☐ the park
☐ the post office   ☐ the post office
☐ the police station   ☐ the police station

The presentation in the video programme of the information given above is highly stylised: a studio setting, with a great deal of pointing to indicate directions. The viewing guide attempts to recapture the relative relationships by the layout of the answers on the paper.

'Where's the post office, please?' A studio scene from Follow Me, *unit 4*

In contrast, the video film used to present the material in the next viewing guide was taken in the street, using actors to simulate reality. Although the language used is fairly simple, the presentation on video includes background noises, such as traffic, and the many distractions of a street scene.

VIEWING GUIDE

Where's the Grand Hotel?	It's ☐ in North Street ☐ in Market Street ☐ in South Street
Where's Castle Street?	It's ☐ on the left ☐ straight ahead ☐ on the right
Where's the Marble Arch Cinema?	It's ☐ next to the bank ☐ near the park ☐ opposite the park

In both these examples, the choices for the learner are limited. Only one possibility in each set is correct. This can be illustrated with the following example in French, taken from *Action-télé*, a lower-intermediate course produced in the UK. Here is the text with the viewing guide:

Réceptioniste: Madame?
Françoise: Vous avez des chambres?
Réceptioniste: Oui.
Françoise: Je voudrais une chambre pour une personne, avec douche, s'il vous plaît.
Réceptioniste: Pour combien de nuits?
Françoise: Juste une nuit, je suis de passage seulement.
Réceptioniste: Un instant—oui, j'ai encore une chambre.
Françoise: A combien?
Réceptioniste: 100 francs, petit déjeuner compris.
Françoise: Oh, c'est un peu trop cher! Vous n'avez rien de moins cher?
Réceptioniste: Si, mais c'est au 4ᵉ et il n'y a pas d'ascenseur.
Françoise: Ça ne fait rien, je la prends.
Réceptioniste: La chambre 407, voilà la clé.
Françoise: On peut dîner à l'hôtel?
Réceptioniste: Oui, la salle à manger est au rez-de-chassée, au fond du couloir à droite.
Françoise: Merci bien. Oh, est-ce que vous avez des timbres?
Réceptioniste: A 1.60F?
Françoise: Non, c'est pour la Grande Bretagne.

Réceptioniste: Non, je regrette, il faut aller au tabac au coin de la rue. A quelle heure partez-vous demain?
Françoise: Vers 8 heures.

VIEWING GUIDE

Mettez, selon le cas, des croix dans les boîtes:

Françoise demande   avec

Françoise doit payer   □ plus que 100Ff
                        □ 100Ff
                        □ moins que 100Ff

Elle prend la chambre   □ 47
                        □ 107
                        □ 407

Elle part le demain   □ vers 8 h.
                        □ vers 7 h.
                        □ vers 9 h.

The task of selection can be made harder for the learners by presenting the choices in another way. In the three examples above one answer in each set of possible answers was correct. In the following viewing guide, an unknown number of items from a list might be correct. The guide is taken from the *Media Teaching Manual* prepared for *Follow Me*, unit 7; the scene is a customs hall, and a custom officer is examining the contents of the priest's suitcase; the arrangement of the nouns in three distinct groups can lead to further language practice.

VIEWING GUIDE

What's in the priest's suitcase?

□ a bottle of gin	□ soap	□ oranges
□ a bottle of milk	□ milk	□ apples
□ a bottle of medicine	□ whisky	□ clothes
□ a bottle of wine	□ make-up	□ keys
□ a bottle of perfume	□ toothpaste	□ cigarettes
□ a bottle of coca-cola	□ marijuana	□ sandwiches

The use of pictures or diagrams, as in the French example above, can be greatly extended. On the one hand, it is useful for learners who cannot read well enough to understand the choices. For advanced learners, a symbol or picture can be used to represent something too lengthy to describe in words on a viewing guide: for example, a managing director, very angry at an unsatisfactory meeting.

There is of course nothing specific to video about constructing guides for listening, reading, or other sorts of watching activities. Worksheets similar to these would be equally valid with many other teaching aids. However, they serve to show how attention can be focused on certain items in a video sequence, without distracting the learner too much by requiring lengthy answers.

When a viewing guide has been completed, it can serve as an *aide mémoire* to the learner for future work in the classroom. For example, in a lesson subsequent to the one when the guide was completed, the teacher might need to recall the information to initiate a new teaching sequence. Not only do all the learners have their own note of what happened, but the viewing guide also serves to remind the whole class, at the same time, of the video presentation. In this way, the class focuses easily on the matter in hand, and gains from the reminder of the shared experience.

Viewing guides are also useful for private work by individual learners or groups of learners. The learners can work with the video on their own, completing the guides. When discussing the contents with the teacher later, attention is again well focused on the video presentation. The same is true concerning broadcast language programmes; many of the viewing guides made for *Follow Me* were intended for use at home, during the broadcast on television of the language programmes. In class, the teacher could then follow up the work that all the learners had done simultaneously, but separately.

There are obvious reasons why these guides should be simple if learners are using them without any help from a teacher or fellow learner. In self-study, it is important to feel confident, successful, and that progress is being made. The viewing guides are not meant to test progress, but encourage it; the construction of the viewing guides reflects this. But there are also valid reasons for viewing guides in the classroom being easy, relative to the language level of the learners. Firstly, they are not meant to detract from the main viewing of the whole video presentation. More importantly, however, learners must be given tasks which they can accomplish – especially if they are not used to working with video equipment for language learning. As mentioned in chapter 1, learners must feel at ease working with this medium, and be assured that it is a positive gain for learning.

More details of the classroom use of viewing guides are given in chapter 3.

2.3   Watching and listening for cues

Asking the learners to watch and/or listen for specific things or language items provides active viewing that is guided yet more open-ended than the worksheets illustrated in section 2.2. The learners are given a cue, and during the presentation they have to write down examples that are relevant.

Verbal cues

In many courses in business English, for example, there are sections of video film showing the language of discussion and argument. Learners might have a cue sheet asking them to write down examples of language which shows that the speaker is
– expressing disagreement
– interrupting
– expressing disbelief or doubt.
This list of cues is based on language functions. In watching and listening for examples, the learners will be greatly helped by the paralinguistic information that the video film carries. Not only the facial expressions and gestures of the speaker help, but also those of the listeners, the other participants in the communication.

This type of activity can be extended into group work. Different learners focus on different aspects of the communication; the results which each gets are then pooled and discussed. For example, in episode 9 of *The Bellcrest Story* (an advanced course in business English) the two main characters have a short discussion in which there are obvious tensions. Business worries and the need for immediate action are making both the chairman and the marketing manager nervous and a little unhappy. The learners could watch this scene in groups of three, each member of the group having a different cue sheet:

Learner A	Learner B	Learner C
As you watch the sequence, note down examples of: - displeasure - disappointment - optimism	As you watch the sequence, note down examples of: - agreement - disagreement - pessimism	As you watch the sequence, note down examples of: - direct commands - indirect commands - resignation

The first two cues for each learner are language functions: the learner is asked to listen out for the speech exponents that express the functions. Intonation patterns, tone of voice, and the vital paralinguistic information will provide further clues. The last cue is an attitude of mind, perhaps; but the same aural and visual clues will help the learner.

If we take on the task of Learner C, and look at just one utterance by the chairman, we can find three commands:

Maurice Downes (Chairman): I'll need the information from that market study for the next board meeting. And I'll need as many other facts and figures as you can give me. You'll need to move fast.

The indirect commands become increasingly urgent, as the chairman tells the marketing manager that he wants the information, some other facts and figures, and he wants them all quickly. But the lexis and structures as presented on this page are open to a wide range of interpretations: disappointment; fear for the future; resignation at events to come. For many learners from cultures outside English-speaking domains, these different interpretations have to be studied and imitated. In later chapters, there are several suggestions for providing this type of practice with similar material.

At a lower level of language competence, learners can listen for specific language items. The notes to the German programme *Wie sagt man . . .?* suggest the following viewing task. However, as quite detailed listening is called for, this task should be carried out on the second or third showing.

Im Park
Alle: Hallo!
Klaus: Was macht ihr denn hier?
Sabine: Wir gehen zum Schwimmbad. Und ihr?
Christof: Wir gehen zum Sportverein.
Klaus: Kommt ihr zu unserer Party?

Tina:	Wann ist die Party denn?
Klaus:	Samstag Abend.
Tina:	Und wo?
Klaus:	Bei Christof im Garten, wenn das Wetter schön ist.
Sabine:	Und wer kommt?
Christof:	Na alle! Christof, Christine, Michael, Thomas und Birga. Die kennst du alle.
Sabine:	Wollen wir gehen?
Tina:	Ja, gut. Wann fängt die Party an?
Christof:	So um sechs.
Sabine:	Habt ihr auch zu essen, oder sollen wir etwas mitbringen?
Thomas:	Ja, vielleicht könnt ihr etwas Kartoffelsalat oder Chips mitbringen.
Sabine:	Gut. Und ein paar Flaschen Kola?
Klaus:	Ja, prima.
Tina:	Hast du gute Musik? Sollen wir ein paar Platten mitbringen?
Klaus:	Hast du die neuste Platte von Pink Floyd?
Tina:	Ja. Gut, ich bringe die Platte mit.
Christof:	Also ihr kommt, ja?
Tina: Sabine: Klaus:	Ja, gut. Das wird sicher eine gute Party.
Sabine:	Also, bis Samstag Abend um sechs.
Alle:	Tschüss!

VIEWING GUIDE

> *Arranging a time for a meeting*
> Underline those time expressions you hear in the film:
>
> Samstag Nachmittag. Morgen Vormittag.
> Heute Nachmittag. So gegen vier Uhr.
> Samstag Abend. Sonntag Nachmittag.
> So um sechs. Bis Sonntag Abend um acht.
> Bis Samstag Abend um sechs. Bis später!

Visual cues

Scenes shot on location bring a wealth of detail and life into the classroom; the video recorder allows these scenes to be used in a great number of ways, some of which lead out beyond the boundaries envisaged by the producers of the film material.

The series *Challenges*, for example, presents six topic areas suitable for young adults who might want to visit Great Britain. One of these topics concerns a community newspaper called *Lower Down*, which is distributed in the area of Wandsworth in South London. The unit contains much of value that can be fully exploited in class with the support materials. But some active viewing with visual cues might be useful work with a

A London street scene from Challenges

class with little experience of life in Great Britain. A classroom discussion on differences in the street life, for example, can be generated by asking the learners to note down things they see which are different in their own country. The opening scenes of theme 5, *Something to Say*, show a volunteer delivering the newspaper *Lower Down* to various parts of Wandsworth. An observant learner could note down the following, for example:

What can you see in the streets of London that is different from things in your own town?

1. Yellow lines on road.
2. Red post boxes.
3. Post office inside a sweetshop.
4. Driving on left!!
5. Car number plates.
6. Trees in street.

The examples given above can of course be adapted to any level. The visual cues can be equally wide ranging. Word fields can be explored: learners note down all vocabulary associated with airports, aircraft and landing that are prompted by a scene in the video. Details of fact that are not relevant to the main theme can be asked for, or noted by the learners in order to quiz their colleagues in groups after the video sequence has been shown; for example:

– what time was it by the station clock when the hero arrived?
– what was the destination of the train he caught?
– where did the lady in the white hat go to after buying a ticket?

Such questions recreate the atmosphere of the movie quiz, known to many viewers from domestic television, and as such will motivate most learners. More significantly, this type of activity illustrates how simply the control of the classroom activity stimulated by the video can be passed to the learners: they choose and ask the questions. A further consideration is that the learners can move away from the closely structured tasks mentioned so far, to more open-ended note-taking.

2.4   Note-taking skills

The ability to take notes is an important skill in everyday life. It is even more important for learners who hope to use a foreign language as a medium for study, for business, or in industry, commerce, or some other vocational field. In some language courses, teaching study skills might be as important as the teaching of the language. The examples given here suggest a gradual introduction to note-taking skills, suitable for learners who need structured practice in the study skill. The examples are also valid for more sophisticated classes, if properly matched to the content of the video materials.

Sorting information

The first essential for good note-taking is knowing what to listen for: what is relevant (and should be noted), and what is peripheral (and may be ignored). Learners unskilled in note-taking need training in how to listen, and what to listen for.

In the following example, the learner has to distinguish who says what. At this stage, no notes are required from the learner, as the listening task is taxing enough at this level of ability in study skills. The cues which must be marked show the learner rather full notes of the sort likely to be required in later exercises. The exercise is from the *Media Teaching Manual* for *Follow Me*; two ladies in a department store are talking about Lowry, the English painter of urban landscapes:

VIEWING GUIDE

> The two ladies are talking about a Lowry print. They give their opinions. Listen to who says what, and mark the boxes.

	one lady says it	both ladies agree with it	nobody says it
I think it's lovely			
I think it's horrible			
I don't like his pictures			
I like all his pictures			
I like his colours			
All his pictures are about hotels			
All his pictures are about factories			

This type of exercise can be rapidly developed, so that the learners are noting who says what. The following example is from *On We Go*, an elementary course for young people. Two teenage girls talk about Mr Yates, the owner of the house where they lodge. Their conversation is overheard by two young men, who are also lodgers, and assume the conversation is about themselves:

Kate: Mr Yates looks great today, doesn't he?
Ann: (*Ann goes to the window.*) Yes, he does.
   (*Mark and Ted are coming downstairs. They hear the girls talking.*)
Ann: Do you like him?
Kate: Yes, I do. Very much.
Ted: (*softly*) Who are they talking about?
Mark: Me.
Ted: You!
Mark: Yes.
Ann: He's very good-looking, too.
Kate: I like his hair.
Mark: They are talking about me!
Ann: He's very polite.
Ted: Polite? That's me – not you.
Kate: And he's funny. He always laughs a lot.
Mark: That's me!
Ann: He's very fit and strong.
Ted: That's me!
Kate: He's very smart. His clothes are very nice. (*Ted and Mark look at their old clothes. They go upstairs to change.*)

Active viewing and comprehension

Ted and Mark go on to disillusionment; but the learner can be making short notes such as the following:

VIEWING GUIDE

List the reasons why the girls like Mr Yates	
Ann	Kate

The same principle can be extended to matching several items in one list with items in another list. The following example in German is taken from *Alles klar* (supplementary material for secondary schools), and concerns the price of fruit in the market.

Auf dem Markt
Lutz: Guten Tag!
Gina: Guten Tag! Wieviel kosten diese Apfelsinsen, bitte?
Lutz: 60 pfg. das Stück.
Gina: Dann zwei Stück, bitte.
Lutz: Ausserdem noch einen Wunsch?
Gina: Ein Kilo Äpfel, bitte.
Lutz: Ein Kilo. Ausserdem noch etwas?
Gina: Ja. Ein Pfund Bananen. Was kostet das?
Lutz: Also, zwei Apfelsinen – 1,20. Ein Kilo Äpfel – DM 3,00. Ein Pfund
        Bananen – 1,90. Das macht zusammen DM 6,10, bitte.
Gina: Bitte schön.
Lutz: Danke schön.
Gina: Auf Wiedersehen!
Lutz: Auf Wiedersehen!

VIEWING GUIDE

Was kostet Obst?			
	60 pfg.	DM3,00	DM1,90
Ein Pfund Bananen			
Apfelsinen pro Stück			
Ein Kilo Äpfel			

22

Learners soon become accustomed to working quickly with viewing guides like these. They can also have two incidental benefits. If copies of the guides are not available for all the class, they can be copied from the overhead projector or the blackboard in a matter of moments. The learners have some easy writing practice – motivated by the desire to see the video presentation. A second benefit is the ease with which these guides can be made up. This means that the pupils themselves can often invent viewing tasks for each other. If they do, it is important that the tasks are kept easy in the early stages of the activity. The main aim of the guides is to help understanding, not test it.

The three examples above are elementary, and related primarily to spoken words. The principle of listening for and sorting information can be applied at any level of language learning. In *The Bellcrest Story* two bankers discuss the question of bank support for rival companies involved in the development of electric speed controls; the scene is at the beginning of episode 9:

Ashburnham: Edward. We can't have Bellcrest and Electrovans competing with each other on the same type of development project. Not with the bank's support, at any rate.

Needham: Precisely. If they insist on competing, which firm will the bank support?

Ashburnham: I'm not sure. Electrovans still depends on one or two big customers.

Needham: Like Beamish Motors, you mean?

Ashburnham: Yes. I see that Beamish is their biggest customer. Forty-five per cent of Electrovans' business goes there.

Needham: Williams admits he's too dependent on Beamish. He'd like to break free, but can't afford to. That's why he wants capital from the bank – to finance expansion.

Ashburnham: When one comes to consider it, the difference between Electrovans and Bellcrest can be seen in the characters of their managing directors.

Needham: Williams and Downes?

Ashburnham: Yes. Under Downes, Bellcrest has become thoroughly sound, but unwilling to take risks. Electrovans, on the other hand, has been more adventurous.

Needham: Electrovans certainly attracts more attention.

Ashburnham: Ah! But perhaps the company lacks the soundness of Bellcrest.

Needham: Electrovans is a forward-looking concern. Look how Donald Williams has pushed ahead with the development of his speed control.

Ashburnham: Doesn't it worry you that the Bellcrest speed control may be revived?

Needham: No, not really. Maurice Downes suspended it five years ago. I don't think he can be very enthusiastic about it now.

At this much more advanced level, the learners can quite properly be asked to list the features and characteristics of the two firms. For the advanced learner, this is not so much practice in the skill of note-taking as such; rather, it is a chance to use the skills he or she has in the foreign language in an easy way.

The written extract printed above cannot convey all the information that this scene contains about Needham, the junior of the two bankers. His manner and bearing strongly suggest that he is against Bellcrest: he seems to be waiting for a chance to pounce on any remark from Ashburnham that the bank would prefer to support Electrovans.

This visual information can also be used by the learners – in this example as a clue to the speakers' attitudes. In other extracts from different video materials, the visual information can of course be the focus for the learners. Learners might be asked to note down what two or three people are doing: who is playing which game, for example; or what does each person buy. Lists of clothing can be made; or places visited; or means of transport; in fact, anything at all that might be presented in a video film.

Guided note-taking

When native speakers take part in communication as listeners, they have the advantage – in most situations – of knowing what to expect in terms of language, and how the communication will proceed. Learners need guidance in this, and note-taking exercises should be prepared to provide this guidance by focusing attention on specific features of language. This preparation can be carried out in a variety of ways. For certain learners, a video sequence might have to be played several times, so that they are thoroughly familiar with the material presented before being asked to make notes. In other situations, other forms of pre-work will mean that the film sequence can be shown for note-taking at first viewing. Whatever method is used, the aim is to make the learners aware of what is to be listened for. This is very easily done with cues on the worksheet, as in the following example.

It is taken from *ESP Travel and Tourism*, an advanced course based on the English of those topic areas. The video sequences were designed for classroom – as opposed to broadcast – use. Generally speaking, the scenes are real-life situations: unscripted, with the roles being taken by employees of a large travel firm. The note-taking task is one that reflects the interests of the likely target group of learners using the materials: writing down the details of a holiday booking. In the video sequence, a booking clerk has to refer to a colleague for information to answer a telephone enquiry about a certain holiday. The colleague in turn has to telephone head office for further information, which is then relayed to the

booking clerk. The booking clerk then gives the client the relevant information. Watching this scene learners can fill out a worksheet such as
this:

VIEWING GUIDE

A holiday taken off sale

A. date: 3rd January
    destination/region: Costa Blanca
    town: Benidorm
    no. of nights: 3
    hotel: Ruidor
    departure from: Luton
    holiday number: A1039
B. reasons for being on bar 3-4 nights → 7 (more saleable)
    On sale at 9.30 next day.
C. explanation to client flight alteration – try at 9.30 tomorrow.

It is likely that employees in the travel industry who use these materials
will also have their own company-specific forms that are used to collect
such information; these could be used instead of worksheets to make the
exercise more relevant to the learners and their interests.

The built-in structure of this sequence means that there is ample opportunity for the learners to check the answers noted, as most of the information is repeated. The booking clerk asks her colleague; the colleague puts
the problem to head office, and then tells the booking clerk the explanation; the booking clerk then edits the explanation for the client. This
sequence is interesting, as it shows how access to total understanding is
made through several layers of comprehension. The first level of
comprehension here is to understand the data presented – that is, part A
of the worksheet. Apart from the value that there is in having the students
fill out their own company forms there is little of lasting interest here. But
part B offers scope for group work and class discussion about similar
things in the learners' own experience. What holidays have been
rearranged in the company? What makes a holiday saleable? The last
part of the transcript shows how Maureen, the manageress, passes the
information from Control to the telephonist, Jan James:

Control: Hello? Well actually this is on a temporary bar. The 4-nights are also
            on bar. What we are actually doing is converting 3- and 4-night seats

Active viewing and comprehension

into 7-nights, to make them more saleable. However, 3- and 4-nights will probably be back on sale tomorrow morning.

Maureen: OK, lovely. Thanks very much indeed. Thank you. Byebye. Right. What's happened, the 3- and 4-night is off sale at the moment. What they are doing, they're joining some 3- and 4-night holidays together to make a 7-night, and that's going to take them overnight to do it. But if the client would like to phone tomorrow morning then hopefully it'll be back on sale at 9.30.

Jan James: OK. Thanks.

Maureen: All right? But it's just to improve saleability on the holidays, the 7-night holidays, which seem to be a little bit more popular than the weekends. All right?

Jan James: OK. Fine. Hello? Well, it seems as though the 3- and 4-night holidays are off sale until at least 9.30 tomorrow morning. Our programme control department altered something on the flight. If you would like to try again tomorrow morning, it could be back on sale then. OK. Fine. Thanks for calling.

The third level of analysis concerns language only. Jan James is speaking to outsiders, who do not need to know the details of the firm's internal arrangements to sell more holidays. For this reason she uses the language of the trade: 'Our programme control department altered something on the flight.' Being able to use this professional half-truth is a quite specific language aim for the target group of this video presentation. A surprisingly high proportion of teachers of English (including native speakers) miss this language point when watching a video presentation, unless their attention is drawn to it in advance. This illustrates the need for guided viewing even at an advanced level.

However, a major attraction of the video recorder in the language classroom is the facility to have pauses when one wishes, and to review sequences just seen.

Using the pause button and review facilities

In the next example, the video recorder is used as an audio tape recorder is often used: a pause button stops the tape; and the tape can then be played on, or rewound for replay. For teachers with no experience of working with video recorders, this offers an easy introduction to the machinery (as do the first examples in the next chapter). On most video recorders, however, using the pause button means that the picture is held on the television screen, in frozen lack of animation. The pause button is often referred to as a 'freeze frame' button.

The following material from *Follow Me*, unit 14, was filmed in a street in an English town; the first speaker is using a public telephone box; he – and the learners – must listen to and note the directions. The guide is from the *Media Teaching Manual*:

VCR plays
Brian: Hello, Derek?
Derek: Yes.
Brian: Derek, it's Brian.
Derek: Hello, Brian. Where are you?
Brian: I'm in Brenton High Street. How do I get to your house?
Derek: Go down the street 500 yards and you'll come to a big supermarket. Turn right there.

Pause button: learners write short notes:

> 500 yards
> supermarket – right

Frame release

Brian: Right at the supermarket. And then?
Derek: Then you go straight on for about one mile and you'll come to a turning on the left.
Brian: One mile. Then turn left.

Pause button: learners write more notes:

> 500 yards
> supermarket – right
> one mile – straight
> turn left

Frame release

Brian: And then?
Derek: My house is the fifth house on the right hand side.
Brian: Fifth house on the right. Thank you Derek; I'll see you in a few minutes. Goodbye.
Derek: Goodbye.

Pause button: learners finish notes:

> 500 yards
> supermarket – right
> one mile – straight
> turn left
> house – 5th on right

Rewind
VCR plays: scene is repeated as learners check notes.
Learners read out the directions from their notes.

Although this type of exercise is complete in itself, in that comprehension can be checked by the adequacy of the notes, there is more value if the exercise can be extended. Using this dialogue and activity as a model, the learners can move on to giving each other telephone directions to various places in the locality, which one of them knows about.

Fuller details of such transfer activities are given in chapter 5.

Free note-taking

The scope for open-ended note-taking is very wide indeed, and need not be restricted to notes in the target language. In many situations, where language is being learned for specific purposes, the learners might be required to take notes in the mother tongue, based on a specialist presentation in the target language. Furthermore, the contents of the notes can be agreed upon, so that the learners share common objectives; or the learners can be free to note whatever is of interest to them personally; an example of this is given in section 2.3.

When language is being learned for specific purposes and learners are making notes on the topic presented, they have a role similar to non-speaking participants in a role play. Their note-taking might mirror activities which they carry out at work. These might include taking part in discussions, listening to lectures, or following demonstrations and explanations of procedures.

For example, in *ESP Business*, a set of materials made on video for classroom use, two company accountants discuss ways of improving the daily cash flow by changing the cheque-cashing arrangements with their bank. The dialogue is unscripted, and provides an opportunity for learners to hear specialist language used in context. The sequence also includes some explanations, told to the camera, about the reasons underlying the decisions which might be made. This material gives interested language learners an excellent chance to familiarise themselves with current practice in the UK; and to exercise the note-taking skills that they might need at meetings with English-speaking colleagues. In section 3.2 we show how comprehension of this text is helped by paralinguistic information – for example, eyebrow movements.

Many language-teaching programmes include instruction in the content matter as well; for example, trainee mechanics are learning not only the language of mechanics, but also about mechanics. Alternatively, there may be occasions when the only video materials available to illustrate or demonstrate an important point are in a foreign language shared by the target audience. In both these cases, it can be legitimate for the learners to make notes in their first language. The nature of the material dictates that comprehension of the demonstration, or whatever, is far more relevant to the learners than the ability or need to use similar language themselves.

Conversely, instructional materials on specialist topics produced in the learners' own language can be adapted for classroom work in the target language. For example, learners might be required to provide their own soundtrack, when the existing soundtrack has been removed. Details of this type of exercise are given in chapter 6.

2.5 Preparations for active viewing

It is clear from most of the above examples that the teacher must be familiar with the video materials before they are used in class, or released to learners for private study. This does not mean that in every case the teacher must preview a complete set of video materials. Of more importance, for teachers' preparation, is access to a transcript of the material, or at least a representative selection from it. The transcript should include all dialogues and voice-overs and commentaries; and, where necessary, a note about the visual elements. These might include references to the use of captions; close-ups of signs, or other significant objects; explanations of 'stage business' or activities carried out without the use of language. With this information, and stills from the sequences to illustrate the style

Switch On *uses the technique of characters addressing the viewer directly, encouraging active viewing*

or idiom of the programmes, teachers can prepare active viewing materials.

Detailed worksheets have to be prepared in advance, and copied for distribution to the class. However, many of the simpler viewing guides can be created on the spot, in the classroom. The learners just copy the columns, or tables, or grid, from the blackboard or overhead projector. While the class is doing this, the teacher can be setting up the tape in the video recorder at the right position. With children, or adult beginners unused to formal learning, a special viewing book or file might be kept, so that the viewing guides and notes are readily available for language work at a later date.

The more detailed uses of the video recorder given in this book assume that teachers are familiar with the construction of programmes and sequences in some detail. Short sections have to be isolated, and used in class with a variety of techniques which are often cued by what happens at precise moments on the screen. As with other teaching materials, teachers become familiar with such details the more often the materials are used. In most cases, video materials will be shared by other teachers in teaching institutions; and by other learners if they are available for self-study in the library mode. Co-operation and careful indexing can bring tremendous benefits to all concerned.

The pressures of language teaching mean that many lessons are given without the preparation that the teacher – or learners – would wish. It can happen that some video materials presented are a new experience for all concerned. Generally speaking, a first showing is not wasted on the learners; they need to be introduced to the topic and the language at some stage, though this may not be the best way of doing it. The teacher should use this opportunity to note down features which can be readily exploited for active viewing. With experience, this becomes relatively easy. Once a teacher is familiar with the style and format of a language series, it is quite easy to make up viewing tasks working from the script.

With certain classes, the level of the material, or the sophistication of the learners regarding video materials, might mean that more advanced work is the first stage after the initial viewing. It might be clear to all concerned that the sequence should be used as a model for a role play; or for detailed listening and note-taking; or for advanced intonation and gesture practice; or for specialist discussion; or whatever the class feel appropriate.

2.6 Summary

The essential features about the techniques outlined in this chapter are that they prepare the learner for what will be presented on the screen; and they encourage participation from the learner through active viewing. Watching a presentation in a foreign language can be a taxing activity. Language learners need help, guidance and reassurance. Teachers can provide these by choosing suitable viewing tasks that are relevant to the learners' needs and abilities.

3 Repetition, prediction, and role play

3.1 Introduction

The main aim of this chapter is to illustrate ways in which video films can be used to encourage oral fluency. A major advantage of using video recorders in class is the controlled presentation of communicative scenes: the teacher or learner can interrupt and replay sequences, freeze the action, and even take away the sound or the vision. Language learners can be invited to join in with part of the video presentation, and to speak in response to the cues they receive. In this way, they can learn to communicate in the target language: presented with a situation, the learners must make any utterance which is valid in that situation.

Detailed examples of this technique are given below; they demonstrate a use of video films which marks the potential of this aid over other classroom teaching aids. However, these examples are preceded by some more simple techniques. Teachers with little experience of using video often prefer to start with a relatively easy task, such as straightforward repetition; as their confidence in handling the equipment increases, so more sophisticated techniques can be practised.

Using the video recorder as a model for repetition may seem a waste of the resources available; after all, audio cassettes provide perfectly good models. This is true in some cases, especially if the repetition exercise is constructed like an audio language laboratory drill. But if the video combines a visual cue with the spoken word – for example, a printed caption – or if the learner is responding to paralinguistic cues in conjunction with the sound, the potential of video films is being used more creatively.

3.2 Simple repetition

Video recorders have a pause button, which can be used simply to stop the film in order to give one or more learners a chance to repeat what has just been said. On some models, particularly older ones, stopping the film means that the picture vanishes from the screen; on most machines, however, the pause button also acts as a freeze frame button, holding the still picture on the screen.

Exact repetition of a given model is not really a communicative exercise. But learners need practice in articulation of new words, or sound groups, or of the intonation patterns of sentence groups. Closely controlled repetition should therefore be seen as a necessary exercise, being used as a precursor to more communicative production exercises.

Vocabulary practice

In *It's Your Turn to Speak*, a video course for beginners, some elementary vocabulary is introduced by showing a picture with the word spoken twice, the second time with an accompanying caption. This can be stopped for repetition either after the first spoken cue; or, with especially weak classes, after the second spoken cue, when there is the added reinforcement of the written cue, that is, a caption saying 'a house', for example. Many teachers would prefer to introduce such vocabulary items in other ways, such as by showing flashcards or magazine pictures, and using their own voice as the model. Both methods are of course valid; but the learner accustomed to the video presentation, and competent to handle the controls of the machine, has a highly motivating presentation of this elementary material available to him or her for self-study and extended private practice.

Practice in context

A more communicative type of controlled repetition is afforded by the following example from *Classroom Video: Functional Sequences*, designed for use with intermediate students:

Asking the way

1   *Street*
    Woman stops man.

Woman:	Excuse me. Could you tell me where the station is?
Man:	Which station?
Woman:	St Pancras.
Man:	Um, go through the shopping centre and then I think you turn left . . . but ask again.
Woman:	OK, thank you. (*Goes into shopping centre. Comes up to man with map.*) Excuse me. Which way is St Pancras?
2nd man:	I'm sorry, I don't know. I'm a stranger here.
Woman:	Oh, OK. (*Comes out of shopping centre. Approaches traffic warden.*) Could you tell me the way to St Pancras Station?
Traffic warden:	Yeah. Turn left at the corner, then go straight on till you come to the second set of traffic lights and it's on your right.
Woman:	Left at the corner, straight on to the second set of lights. Thanks. (*Stops passer-by.*) Excuse me, St Pancras?

| 2nd woman: | Yeah. Go up to the lights and you'll see it across the road on your right. |
| Woman: | Fine. Thanks. (*Comes to main road. Sees St Pancras sign.*) |

The scene lasts for about a minute, and is clearly scripted to show different language exponents of the speech function 'asking the way'. Any phrase or utterance in this short sequence can be used for repetition practice, but with various teaching aims, apart from the immediate problem of correct articulation and pronunciation.

Repetition of the questions put by the woman provides valuable practice for learners. In structural terms, it gives practice in the formation of questions. This is an area of language usage which learners need, and which is frequently taught inadequately in classrooms. In functional terms, the learners are offered variants of the same intention, asking the way. In communicative terms, the learner sees how the language is used appropriately in the situation. The passers-by can be seen, and it is clear that – in this example – language in the same neutral, but polite register, is used with strangers of different sex, different ages, different social status, and so on. For most learners of English, the choice of second-person address forms in the native language is dependent on some or all of these features. On the video film, the presentation of the complete communicative situation means that this information is implicitly stated; the learner can appreciate this aspect of the use of language without detailed explanations. A similar video film in German, for example, would illustrate the different address forms 'du', 'ihr' and 'Sie'.

Repetition of the answers given by the passers-by provides practice of a different kind. The sequence leads up to the giving of the directions. But there are also opportunities for learners to practise expressing their regrets. In the example above, one passer-by definitely does not know where the station is, another passer-by is not completely sure.

In a similar sequence in *Follow Me*, gradations of certainty are introduced in the fourth unit. To the question 'Where's the Grand Hotel?', learners can practise the answers:

– It's in Market Street.
– I think it's in Market Street.
– I'm sorry, I don't know.

The repetition involves not only the words and intonation used, but also the body language which accompanies them. With the response 'I think it's in Market Street', this involves the following:

– knitting the eyebrows;
– rolling up the eyeballs;
– shifting weight from left to right foot;
– raising the outstretched finger of right hand to the chin.

This is difficult to appreciate in writing; and impossible to explain verbally using this language with a class of real beginners. It is easy to imitate from the screen.

Copying gesture and intonation

Paralinguistic features, such as gesture, and suprasegmental features, such as intonation pattern, often lend a meaning to something spoken which cannot be guessed at by seeing the words on the printed page. For example, the words 'I take your point, Paul. I'm sure we all do' could indicate agreement with something just said. But in the extract below, taken from *The Bellcrest Story*, all the remarks made by Downes indicate fairly strong disapproval of the recommendations made by Paul Malone. The scene is a meeting of senior management, and is taken from episode 6:

Malone: Well, there's no doubt about the obvious solution to our short-term problems. That is, to concentrate on the product lines which will bring in the quickest returns and the largest profits.

Downes: Is that what you suggest we do?
Pause button
Learners repeat
Pause button release

Malone: Not exactly. I recommend that we should look after our regular customers as well as possible. But we must pay special attention to those customers who are likely to bring in our long-term profits.

Downes: What's the feeling about Paul's proposal?
Pause button
Learners repeat
Pause button release

Spence: (*To Malone*) Clearly, you want to give priority to those orders which in the short term will yield the smallest return. The latest German orders, for instance.

Malone: It's true that these orders are less profitable than orders for the same products in this country. But our long-term growth will suffer if we lose our overseas customers.

Downes: I take your point, Paul. I'm sure we all do.
Pause button
Learners repeat
Pause button release / Switch off

Learners of business English might like to copy the manner of Downes's speech, as it is characteristic of the way many businessmen conduct meetings with colleagues. However, for many learners of a foreign language there is no need to attempt to emulate native-speaker standards or styles of speech. But for these learners it is nonetheless important to be able to recognise what a native speaker's words are actually communicating. In this example, every native speaker recognises that 'I take your point . . .

I'm sure we all do' . . . will be followed by 'but . . .!' – whether spoken or just implied. This type of recognition and comprehension practice can be introduced using the video film with no sound; some examples of this technique are given in the next chapter.

3.3 Prediction in controlled situations

Although repetition has a place among language-learning exercises, video material is particularly well suited to activities which require predictive speech from learners. Using the visual cues on the screen, and parts of the spoken dialogue, learners must predict what is going to be said. This is a much more closely structured activity than speculation; in speculative exercises the learners can draw on all their knowledge of the language to discuss hypothetical happenings, or to give explanations and reasons for things. Some of these types of activities are discussed in chapter 4. Our concern here is predictive speech closely related to situations, as the following two examples show.

The cues that lead the learner to decide what to say in these exercises spring from the situation presented by the video materials. The learner is required to respond to the situation. What the learner says is not based on a direct model, as is the case with repetition exercises. Rather the learner, within the controlled framework of the situation, is required to make an utterance which is valid for the situation. The learners must draw on their communicative ability to express themselves in a way appropriate to the situation, without a model being supplied. This is possible even with beginners. The example below is from the *Media Teaching Manual* for *Follow Me*, unit 7; the learners' possible answers, taken from a sample of the class each time, can be varied, and different from the response given by the actor on the screen; in this example, the scene was played for comedy by the actors:

Customs officer:	Good morning, sir. Are these your suitcases?
	Pause button
Learners:	Yes / Yes, they are / Yes, that's right.
	Pause button release
Priest:	Yes, they are.
Customs officer:	And is this your suitcase?
	Pause button
Learners:	Yes, it is / Yes.
	Pause button release
Priest:	Yes, it is.
Customs officer:	Would you open this one, please.
Priest:	Yes.
Customs officer:	Excuse me, what's this?
	Pause button

Learners:	Wine / It's wine / It's a bottle of wine.
	Pause button release
Priest:	It's a bottle. It's a bottle of wine.
Customs officer:	And this? What's this?
	Pause button
Learners:	Perfume / It's perfume / It's a bottle of perfume.
	Pause button release
Priest:	It's a bottle too. A bottle of perfume.
Customs officer:	What's that?
	Pause button
Learners:	Soap / It's soap / That's soap.
	Pause button release
Priest:	Soap.
Customs officer:	Soap?
Priest:	Yes, it's soap.
Customs officer:	And what's this?
	Pause button
Learners:	Toothpaste / It's toothpaste / That's toothpaste.
	Pause button release
Priest:	It's toothpaste. Toothpaste.
Customs officer:	And these? What are these?
	Pause button
Learners:	Cigarettes / They're cigarettes.
Teacher:	(*To screen*) These are cigarettes.
	Pause button release
Priest:	Cigarettes. These are cigarettes.
Customs officer:	And these?
	Pause button
Learners:	Keys / They're keys.
	Pause button release
Priest:	These are keys. They're keys.

The interjection by the teacher 'These are cigarettes' is required in this example to avoid confusion amongst the learners. The teacher can validly say 'These are cigarettes', if he or she is standing near the screen and pointing. From classroom seats, learners need 'those are' or 'they're'.

Practice of this type serves as an excellent introduction to role play, and in section 3.4 an example shows how the bridge from predictive speech to role play is made.

3.4   Reacting to situations

The setting for the dialogue above – in a customs hall – determined the type of situation presented to the learners, and consequently the type of language required of them. In this case, mainly lexical items referring to the things in the suitcase. The following example shows how, at the same elementary level, learners can be asked to give responses that are more dependent on the situation. The language being practised is that of informal greetings. An American couple greet an English friend in this scene from *It's Your Turn to Speak*; the learners take the role of the visitor who arrives in New York by train:

Sam: That's the train, there. There he is. Ted! Hi, Ted! How are you?
                   Pause button
Learners: I'm fine, thanks. / Fine, thank you. / Very well, thank you. How are you?
                   Pause button release
Ted: I'm fine, thanks. How are you?
Sam: I'm fine.
Ted: It's good to see you again.
Sam: Thanks. You look well.
                   Pause button
Learners: Thanks. / Thank you, so do you. / Thanks. You look good too.
                   Pause button release
Ted: Thanks. So do you.
Sam: Thanks. This is my wife, Alice, Ted.
Alice: Hi. Hello.
                   Pause button
Learners: Hello, pleased to meet you. / Hi. / Hello, Alice.
                   Pause button release

'It's good to see you again.' A scene from It's Your Turn to Speak

Ted: Hello, Alice.
Alice: How was your trip?
            Pause button
Learners: It was fine, thank you. / Fine. / It was very good, I enjoyed it a lot. / Fine, thanks.
            Pause button release
Ted: Very fine, thank you.
Alice: Welcome to New York.
            Pause button
Learners: Thank you. / I'm very pleased to be here. / Thanks – I'm very excited, etc.
            Pause button release
Ted: Thanks.
Sam: Let me take your bags, Ted.
Ted: Oh, here. You take that one.
Sam: OK.
Alice: It's this way.

The simplicity of the language in these examples serves to show that the principle can be applied to all language levels. From the first language lessons, learners can be guided to use whatever language they have at their command appropriately. In this way, situationally relevant communicative competence can be developed, rather than rote learning of language models from textbooks and tapes of drills. The appropriate use of language in a given situation underlies role-playing exercises, which are a logical extension of exercises in predictive speech.

3.5 Role play

If learners are to use language appropriately in situations, it is important that they understand what the situation is about as quickly as possible. Video presentations of scenes that learners should use as a model provide an excellent way of explaining all the aspects of a communicative situation. To set the scene for a role play based on the example from *Follow Me*, in a customs hall, the teacher need do no more than play the tape through. There is then likely to be little or no need for explanations which tell the learner that a customs officer is searching through the luggage of an embarrassed priest, who has arrived in the UK from a trip abroad. Many explanations such as this are an intrusion into valuable class time, and are more especially so if they are given in the learners' native tongue – which is often the case.

The presentation of the scene on video has two other important advantages, compared with conventional explanations of a proposed role play. After seeing a model acted out in front of them, all the learners have a clear idea of what is required. The constraints that operate, or the limits within which the action should be contained, can be made quite explicit by reference to the video model. The second major advantage concerns the learners' self-assurance. For a wide variety of reasons, many learners are shy of role playing in front of their fellow learners. The video model provides a cover for these learners. Rather than trying – and possibly failing – to act the scene in their own way, learners can consciously act like the actors in the video presentation. This element of mimicry means that their own personalities are distanced from the role play, which increases the learners' confidence. Of course, in the very early stages of learning a language in a class with a teacher, some learners may be too shy even to imitate an actor. In the customs scene, such learners can be introduced to role play by taking walk-on parts with no speaking – in this example, the other passengers who walked through the green channel without a challenge from the customs officer. But most classes should lose any reluctance to role play once the technique has been introduced and the right climate for co-operative language learning established.

Role play is generally an activity which takes place at the end of any particular teaching unit. The learners need to be sure of vocabulary and structures likely to be required, so that they can perform as fluently as possible. Presenting a model on the video helps in the ways outlined above. If the content of the model is too difficult for immediate understanding, then a guided viewing exercise should be used. To familiarise learners with vocabulary associated with travellers' suitcases, for example, the viewing guide illustrated in section 2.2 could be used. But if we assume that adequate preparation is done, a role play based on a video model can be introduced in the following stages:

Stage 1   Presentation of the scene on video (with guided viewing and comprehension checks as appropriate).

Stage 2   Replay of the scene on video, with pauses for predictive viewing (as detailed in the two examples above).

Stage 3   Replay of the scene on video; one or more learners takes a spoken role, replacing the voice of the speaker on video.

Stage 4   Learners make notes of vocabulary or structures required, and assemble any props or items needed for the role play.

Stage 5   Role play of a scene by learners (which can be filmed if a video camera is available).

4 Gesture, register, and structures

4.1 Visual cues for comprehension

Paralinguistic features form an important part of communication. Through arm movements, facial gestures, and eye contact speakers convey meaning to their dialogue partners. Often gestures and mime can carry the whole meaning; the words are unnecessary. For language learners the ability to recognise, understand and perhaps use these features of the target language is an integral part of achieving communicative fluency.

In language-learning systems spoken dialogues – either authentic or made-up – are preserved for study by the learners, and presented to them, in many diverse ways. We can group these into three broad categories: printed materials; audio materials; and audio-visual materials. Each of these modes has distinct advantages and disadvantages when compared with the others.

Printed texts are by far the most common way of preserving spoken dialogues. In the vast majority of cases, the print implies paper: books, pamphlets, worksheets. Increasingly, however, it implies storage by means of an electronic medium with facilities for a print-out as necessary. For example, the information stored on a floppy disk as part of a computer system can be called up as print on a television screen at any time. Or the same information can be transferred to paper, as is common with word processors. However printed, these materials have the great advantage of permanence. The learner can keep the text for prolonged study. The language content of the text can be subjected to detailed study: syntax and morphology can be studied at leisure, for example.

However, printed materials give us little information about *how* the language is spoken. This is clear from the need to use italics or underlining (as in the previous sentence) to indicate stress or emphasis. Many printed dialogues also include 'stage instructions' to help make meaning clear; these are normally in brackets: (angrily); (running to the window).

Audio recordings offer the language learner much more information about the spoken language. Depending on the quality of the recording, phonetic features are available for analysis or use as a model. Furthermore, prosodic features – such as pitch, rhythm, tempo and loudness – are also apparent. These together mean that the learners' potential for understanding the full communicative meaning of something spoken is greatly increased. However, audio recordings are transient. Once an utterance has been made the tape progresses on into the dialogue. There is no chance to 'glance back' as one can with written materials. The only possibility is to replay the tape.

Another disadvantage of audio recordings is that any gains made in authenticity tend to increase the difficulty of comprehension. Some learners are taught language entirely by audio/oral means; the emphasis is only on listening and speaking. For these learners audio tapes may present no problem. But the vast majority of language courses also include reading components, and usually writing components too. For these learners it is generally accepted that reading a dialogue for comprehension is easier than hearing the same dialogue on audio tape.

A similar comparison can be made between audio recordings and audio-visual recordings. An audio-visual recording with moving pictures – such as film, television or video – offers the phonetic and prosodic advantages of audio, as well as the paralinguistic information provided by the visual element. This means that at any given level of language competence, the learner's potential for comprehension is greatly increased if the visual information is included in the presentation.

To illustrate this, we can look at the following example taken from *ESP Business*. It is from a short sequence between native speakers who are discussing the cash flow in a large organisation. One of the speakers says:

'It's going to be around about £600,000, but I think – bearing in mind towards the end of the year the money does come in that much faster anyway, on, erm, the capital UK accounts – there shouldn't be any problem in meeting that out of our current daily bankings.'

Few course writers would include such a sentence in dialogue written specially for a textbook. In transcription from a video scene, the sentence is quite difficult to read. The value of the transcript is as a point of reference when working with the video. If the same sentence were heard on an audio tape, the level of language competence required by the learners for comprehension would be far higher than that required when watching it on video tape. This is because the difficult syntax spoken by the native speaker is marked and aided by various paralinguistic features. The suggestion of uncertainty at the beginning of the text, followed by the concession to the increased cash flow at the end of the year with some normal hesitation while searching for words all lead to a long sentence made understandable by the fact that we can see the speaker.

Visual cues can aid comprehension of more than just words. They are often most meaningful as indicators of mood, emotions, or temperament. An appreciation of the psychological aspects of communication is an integral part of language learning.

Businessmen communicate with body language. A scene from The Bellcrest Story

In unit 8 of the *The Sadrina Project* there is a short scene between the managing director of a tour company (Bill Marsden) and one of his assistants (Ron Howells). During the scene, Ron Howells carries out a large number of non-verbal activities. These include:
– opening desk drawers;
– sorting out files;
– shuffling through papers;
– walking away from Bill Marsden while Bill is talking;
– walking away from Bill Marsden while he is talking himself;
– sorting documents on the desk.
This visual information can be exploited with the learners in a variety of ways. A simple task is to ask them to note down how many things they see Ron Howells doing in the scene, apart from speaking to his boss. A task requiring interpretation is likely to prove more valuable, however, in terms of understanding what is happening. The scene can be played to the learners without the sound – simply by turning off the sound volume control on the television monitor. The learners watch the sequence, and are asked to interpret what Ron Howells is communicating by his behaviour.

Non-British native speakers of English feature in The Sadrina Project

This type of exercise teaches more than just language. It also offers to the learners insights into the whole communicative process. For example, through his actions Ron Howells may be communicating to us in a quite different way than he is communicating to the boss, Bill Marsden. To him, Ron Howells is trying to give the impression of being very busy, of being preoccupied with other matters, and that the topic under discussion is of little consequence. However, it is clear to the viewer (especially when the visual cues are seen in conjunction with the spoken dialogue) that Ron Howells is trying to avoid a face-to-face confrontation with the boss. In the story of *The Sadrina Project* he is one of the villains of the piece; in the scene he is expecting – and trying to avoid – a severe rebuke from the boss. A second feature of this type of exercise is the scope it gives to the learners for further discussion. It is likely that not every learner will interpret the visual cues correctly. A mistake of interpretation, however, is different from a mistake in language. Language errors are often quite clearly incorrect; the teacher or other class members can provide a 'right answer'. In matters of interpretation there are many more degrees of rightness and wrongness. With a class who have given an inaccurate interpretation, it can be most useful to discuss the aspects of the context which need to be changed in order to make their interpretation more accurate. Communication involves more than just language; and that communication can vary according to the context. Moreover, within any given communicative context, language learning involves more than just words, syntax and meaning. It also involves the full range of human emotions, moods and relationships.

4.2 Differing register in differing situations

A lawyer who speaks in court to the judge and jury uses a different type of language when relaxing with family and friends at home. A shop assistant in a department store will usually speak to customers more formally than he or she does to friends in the store. Different social situations require different language; a competent speaker must choose the most appropriate register of language for any situation.

Many language learners are able to achieve reasonable fluency and accuracy in the target language, in the context of the classroom. The same learners then go on to make mistakes in personal dialogue with native speakers, or when drafting written correspondence. The mistakes these learners make are not the formal mistakes of grammar; in strictly grammatical terms, there may be no errors of syntax or concord, for example. However, in terms of the situation in which the language is used, the learner is saying or writing something which is inappropriate.

Exercises in appropriateness can easily be developed from video presentations of communication. In the native language the normal language learner has enough competence to understand why certain utterances are too polite, too vulgar, too formal, or too full of slang expressions to meet certain situations. The parameters which determine the appropriateness of a remark are, of course, more than linguistic. They involve the full range of paralinguistic features and inter-personal relationships which have been discussed in previous sections. These can be presented to the learner in a controlled fashion, using the flexibility of the video recorder in class.

For example, in *Bid for Power* a good model for the language of international negotiation for businessmen is provided in many of the scenes. In one sequence the chairman of the National Development Agency wants to gain some time to consider options other than those being proposed to him by the representative of a major multi-national company. At one stage he interrupts the main flow of discussion to ask: 'Can we perhaps adjourn the discussion until tomorrow?' This scene can be exploited by the teacher in a variety of ways, for example:
- changing the setting;
- changing the dialogue partners;
- changing the ages of the participants;
- changing the relative business roles of the speakers.

Bid for Power *dramatises the problems of a developing country*

For learners who are less capable of producing good English, alternatives can be suggested to them by the teacher. In the following example based on the same sequence, the task for the learner is to rank the alternatives given in order of appropriateness.

Mark the boxes (a), (b) or (c) to show how you rank the sentences:

(a) We'll talk about it tomorrow, OK?   more polite ☐

(b) I wonder if it would be at all possible
    to make some arrangement whereby   the same ☐
    we could look into this matter further
    tomorrow?

(c) Do you think we could follow this   less polite ☐
    point up tomorrow?

Assessing the learners' answers will lead to the same sort of discussion as outlined above.

Having made the learners aware of the differences in communicative value of the utterances, the sentences can also be used for language analysis. The learners can be given insights into the lexical and syntactic features of the utterances. For example, with guidance the following lists could be drawn up by the learners working in small groups:

register	language features
formal and/or polite	conditionals (e.g. 'could'; 'might') adverb phrases (e.g. 'really'; 'at all possible') complex sentences (e.g. 'if' clauses)
neutral	simple sentences
informal and/or rude	ellipsis (e.g. 'tomorrow, OK?') slang

The following two methods would be suitable for learners at different levels of language ability. If the learners are aware of the role of style and register in language, and are able themselves to produce good English, the teacher can invite alternatives to the above sentence. The alternative must match the situation as presented on the video in terms of politeness, degree of formality and language register.

Correct responses from the learners will reinforce their understanding of the situation, and their ability to function effectively in English in such a situation. Such a response might be: 'Do you think we could follow this point up tomorrow?'

Incorrect suggestions from the learners can also be turned to good advantage. As in the example in section 4.1, the learners can be led into a discussion about the whole communicative situation. A suggestion such as: 'We'll talk about it tomorrow, OK?' can be used to demonstrate to the learner the type of language that can be used when the speakers are on a less formal basis than in the video presentation. A catalogue of necessary changes can be set up by the learners in discussion, which indicate how the situation might be changed to match the utterance: role of syntax, ellipsis, and similar language features in communication. The first choice given above (a) uses colloquial abbreviations, a non-interrogative syntax, and the casual phrase 'OK', indicating informality, possibly intimacy – and, with certain intonations, finality. In the second example, the use of modal verbs, elaborate syntax, and adverb phrases indicates the elaborate speech of a high register and a degree of formality inappropriate for the situation. The third example given is in length, choice of lexis and use of syntax, similar to the original. In this way, the learners can develop an awareness of the different styles and register of a language.

4.3 Controlled language practice

A necessary step to communicative fluency is the practice of discrete language items. Fluency is the ability of the learner to assemble the various bits and pieces of a language system at will, in order to meet the demands of a particular situation. The flexibility of the video recorder offers a wide variety of opportunities for controlled language practice in the classroom. The intrinsic interest in the televisual presentation adds greatly to motivation; but there are potential drawbacks. The richness of the material might mean that learners are being expected to produce language more difficult than the teaching point being shown to them. For example, it is easy to stop a video sequence at any point and ask the learners what has happened / will happen / could happen. Learners can be expected to respond sensibly only if the necessary pre-teaching has taken place, or their language confidence is already at a sufficiently high level.

Narrative recall

One of the easiest uses of the video recorder in class is to stop the tape, and ask the learners what happened in the story up to that point. In English this will elicit from the learners in a controlled way the verb forms associated with the narrative:

simple past – used to recount the main events in the story;
past perfect – used to refer to something which had occurred earlier in the story;
past continuous – used for background description.

Following this model, a learner might recount the sequence in *The Sadrina Project* quoted in section 4.1 as 'When Bill Marsden *came* into the office, Howells *was sorting out* papers on his desk. Marsden *was* angry because he *had instructed* Howells to . . .'

Asking learners to retell the story of a previous unit is, of course, a good way of starting any lesson. But narrative recall can also serve other language-learning uses. In German, for example, different tense forms may be used to express the past, depending on the mode of expression: oral or written. Narrative recall can thus be used to provide controlled practice in tense forms. In the classroom, oral practice can be given in which the present perfect is used: 'Ja, die zwei Jungs *sind* in die Stadt *gegangen*, und *haben* dort ein paar Freunden *getroffen* . . .'

As a follow-up activity, either as individual homework or perhaps as a group project, the narrative can be written up. The same scene might then be represented by: 'Am Samstag Nachmittag *gingen* Harald und Klaus-Peter in die Stadt. Die *trafen* sich dort mit ein paar Freunden . . .'

This second activity shows how follow-up classwork can move away

from the video presentation. Narrative recall can form the basis of many classroom activities, such as quizzes. For example, learners can make notes on the sequence themselves, and try to catch out members of the opposing teams with questions such as:
- What did the man wearing a blue tie buy in the shop?
- Who opened the restaurant door first?
- What happened after the dog ran away?

Depending on the type of video sequence shown, the learners are able to exercise a little initiative and fantasy of their own. Some language-teaching materials, of course, draw on the learners' liking for the absurd. In *We Mean Business* the central character is an eccentric placed in a business environment – humorously, as everything he does is at odds with accepted practice. Learners often fasten on details and events which seem to escape the notice of coursebook writers and many teachers. Some detailed examples of such follow-up activities are given in the next chapter.

Reported speech

Telling a third party what someone else has said is an everyday occurrence for native speakers in any language. For learners of a foreign language, reported speech often causes great difficulty. Shifts in tense forms, concord between tenses, the need to recast pronominal forms, the necessary introduction of new lexical items – all these factors can make reported speech difficult.

A simple way to practise reported speech is to play a dialogue, and ask the learners who said what. The following scene is taken from *Classroom Video: Functional Sequences*:

Photo booth in station
Woman comes out of booth. Waits for photos. Man goes in.
Man: Can you tell me how this works?
Woman: Yes, I think so. You put your money in here. Then the light flashes four times. Don't move until it finishes . . . oh and pull the curtain round.
Man: Thank you. (*Puts money in. Four flashes. Comes out.*)
Woman: Now you must wait four minutes and your photos come out here. Don't touch them till they're dry.
Man: Thank you very much. Very kind of you.
Woman: Not at all. A pleasure.

This might be reported by a learner in the words which follow; the italics indicate specific teaching/learning points:

Learner: The man wanted to use a photo booth at the station, and he asked the woman *if she could* tell him *how it worked*. The woman *told him how it worked*, so the man . . .

Teacher: What did she actually say?

Learner: Well, she told him *where to put the money in* and *explained* that the light flashes four times. She told him about the curtain, and *not to move until it finished*.

Teacher: Go on.

Learner: She told him that he *would have to* wait for four minutes, and she showed him *where* the photos *would come out*. She said *you shouldn't* touch them till they're dry. Then *he thanked* her and she went away.

It is clear from the italics what the main points of language practice might be. If we conjecture a class which are fairly good at reported speech, but need specific practice in the use of the modals, then we can see how reporting speech in such a tightly controlled situation yields the target language. In this sense, the exercise illustrated here is worthwhile. But, as it stands, there is little communicative value in the exercise.

One of the reasons why the communicative value is so low is because the made-up responses are inappropriate to the scene quoted. Reporting speech is more than rephrasing what somebody else has said. A more valid task concerned with instructions on how to operate a photo booth is to take notes, and be sure that one follows the correct sequence.

To create the necessary conditions for communicative reported speech, one participant in the dialogue must want to know what someone else has said. If a dialogue takes place between A and B, then C can justifiably ask B what A has said.

One way of creating an information gap (between B and C) is to follow up the video sequence with a role play. The key point is to introduce into the role play somebody who has not seen or understood the original video sequence. In *Classroom Video: Viewing Comprehension* there is a scene between a doctor and a character called Jim who is presented to the viewer as a possible hypochondriac. The scene is a normal doctor–patient interview, and Jim is suffering from nothing more than a 24-hour virus. A role play can be set up as follows with a class that is divided into three groups.

Group A have the role of observers, identifying with the doctor, but also checking on the content of the subsequent role play. The members of group A are likely to be the learners with the best level of language competence.

Group B identify with Jim. They too have to take notes on what the doctor says; they will then have to retell the information to the members of group C.

The scene is shown to groups A and B only. The members of group C are occupied with other work. After the scene has been shown, group C rejoin the whole class, which is then split into small groups of three. In each group is one member of groups A, B and C.

In each group, C has to find out from B (Jim) what the doctor (A) said. This is the easiest language role, although persistent questioning may be needed to get all the details.

The transcript of this scene is given below.

At the Health Centre

Jim walks along corridor. Sign switched from 'Wait' to 'Enter'. Knocks.

Doctor: Come in! Ah, hello Mr Martin!
Jim: Hello Doctor.
Doctor: How are you?
Jim: Oh, dreadful!
Doctor: Ah dear! And what seems to be the trouble?
Jim: Well I, er . . . last night I felt as if I was going down with a cold, um, and I went into the office this morning and, er, by eleven o'clock I was just feeling dreadful – I had a headache, temperature, throat, glands.
Doctor: Mm. Ah. *(rising)* You and a few thousand others. Time of year I should think . . . *(Feels forehead and glands.)* tender?
Jim: Yes.
Doctor: Ahem. Right. Head back. Open wide, Aaahh!
Jim: Aaaaahhhhhh!
Doctor: Hmmm. Well, nothing serious, it's one of these viruses that are going around, lasts approximately 24 hours. I would suggest that you keep warm over the weekend, plenty of rest, plenty of liquid and I should think you'll be back to work by Monday.
Jim: Monday?
Doctor: Hmmm, yes I should think you'll be perfectly all right.
Jim: Er, you don't think I might need a few more days off?
Doctor: No, I shouldn't think so – if you get a headache over the weekend or you find that you're running a temperature again, just aspirin, paracetamol, whatever you usually like to take – all right?
Jim: Right. Thank you Doctor.
Doctor: Bye.

Speculation

Video is a resource rich in potential to fire the imagination of language learners. With almost any video film learners can be asked to speculate on what will happen next; to interpret what they can see; or to guess at the past events which had led up to the scene being shown. Given the right level of language ability in the learners, such exercises are virtually limitless in scope.

With classes at a lower level of language competence, it may be necessary for teachers to frame questions so that the learners' answers focus on

What happens next in this scene from Follow Me?

particular language features. In English, the following interrogatives and
sentence frames might be used:

simple present	Teacher:	Why does he go into the . . .?
	Learner:	I think he wants to . . .
'going to' future	Teacher:	What do you think she is going to do?
	Learner:	Perhaps she is going to . . .
'will'	Teacher:	What do you think they'll do now?
	Learner:	Well, I think they'll . . .
'if' clauses	Teacher:	What do you think they'll do if (something happens)?
	Learner:	If that happens, then I think they'll . . .
	Teacher:	What do you think they would do if (something happened)?
	Learner:	If that happened, then I think they would . . .
	Teacher:	What could they have done if (something had happened)?
	Learner:	If that had happened, then they could/might have . . .
present perfect	Teacher:	Why do you think the little boy is (crying)?
	Learner:	Perhaps he is sad because he has (lost his money).

These type of exercises can be extended in English or applied in any language. The important point is that the language expected from the learners is within their range of ability. A succession of questions concentrated on the same language point leads learners to repeated practice of that point, but without the obvious sameness of repetitive drills.

In the short outline above, the exploitation of the video sequence is rather teacher-centred. That is to say, the teacher initiates all the questioning in order to elicit the correct language form under consideration. But, as mentioned in the section on narrative recall, it is quite possible to hand the initiative for questioning over to the learners. More details of this technique are given in chapter 5.

Good storytellers create situations where everyone wants to know what happens next. Language teachers can build on this by asking students for more detailed versions of their speculative accounts. This can involve more lengthy oral practice in class, or lead to a wide variety of written projects.

Focus on a language feature

Some examples were given in section 2.3 in which the learners' attention is drawn to particular features of language. The communicative aspects of a video presentation can often make clear to a learner a point of language which is difficult to explain in words alone. In the following example the focus is on second-person address forms.

Speakers of standard English use (and expect to be addressed by) the one form 'you' in normal situations requiring a second-person address. We can ignore here such special usages by shoe-shop assistants: 'Has madam found anything she likes?'. Being accustomed to one form only, English speakers must learn a complex set of socio-linguistic rules if they are to master the second-person address forms in many languages. European languages sometimes (but not always) make a distinction between singular and plural. Distinctions are also made (but not always) according to the degree of intimacy, formality or politeness that is required on the occasion. The table below offers a simplified overview of the second-person address forms in some European languages; there are of course many languages with far more complicated systems.

At some stage in the language learners' progress, the rules which govern the choice of address pronoun have been made specific. But video presentations of the language can show the use of these address forms in context. Because of the visual component of the presentation the various dialogue partners can be clearly seen. The learners can be led to note down the differences in usage, and discuss among themselves what rules might govern the system. In *Wie sagt man . . .?* the learners have to note who is

Address forms in some European languages

	Singular		Plural	
	intimate	*polite*	*polite*	*intimate*
Spanish	tu	Usted	Ustedes	vosotros
German	du	Sie		ihr
Danish	du	De		I
French	tu		vous	
Russian	ti		vi	
Yiddish	du		ir	
Scots Gaelic	tu		su	
Irish Gaelic	tu		sibh	
English	you			

addressed by 'Sie' and who by 'du'. Using their notes they then have to complete the following table. In this way, the learners experience, albeit through the video presentation, the rule systems in action. The learning process is inductive, rather than being rule-governed.

VIEWING GUIDE

Which questions might *you* be asked by	a stranger	a friend
Woher kommen Sie?	✓	
Wo wohnst du hier?		✓
Was machst du hier?		✓
Wie lange bleiben Sie hier?	✓	
Können Sie um 4 kommen?	✓	
Kommst du zu unserer Party?		✓
Haben Sie Lust, Kaffee zu trinken?	✓	

Video presentations can also clarify other points which involve leaping a conceptual gap from the native language into the target language. Examples of this might include:

German — verbs of position (legen, setzen, stellen)
— gender (der, die, das: three designations)
Russian — verbs of motion (chodit', ezdit', nosit', vodit', etc.)
— animate vs. inanimate declension (accusative/genitive case of masculine nouns)
French — cognition (savoir, connaître)
— gender (le, la: two designations).

Focus on lexis

Introducing and teaching individual vocabulary items is a fundamental part of language work in the classroom. A wide range of methods are available to the teacher, together with an equally wide range of techniques. These include drawings on the blackboard or overhead projector; magazine pictures; models or actual objects themselves; definitions in the target language; and so on. Video has the potential of bringing into the classroom a wide range of objects, places, and even concepts, in an easy way, without straining the resources of the average language teacher. The flexibility of the video recorder means that the target lexis can be practised in a number of ways.

To introduce single lexical items, the freeze frame button can be used to focus on one object. The teacher can label the object ('this is a jet'), and the film can be restarted. A variation of this is to play the video tape in slow motion. The teacher labels the objects or actions as they pass on the screen. Such exercises can easily be turned into games and quizzes, with the learners having to recall as many items as possible. This type of activity forms a part of many popular quiz shows on television.

The slow motion technique may also be used to expand vocabulary in related word fields. For example, within the context of international jets a teacher might offer the following commentary; the new vocabulary items are in italics.

'Now here's the jet. This is the *runway*. Now look: the pilot lowers the *undercarriage* and prepares for *touch-down*. The wheels *touch-down* once – you can see the smoke – and then the plane *touches-down* again. (cut to cockpit) The pilot in the *cockpit* is talking to the (cut) *control tower*. The plane *taxis* across the tarmac, and the pilot heads for the *terminal*.'

Learners often wish to know lexical items which are not part of the course syllabus and which have not been included in the course materials. Giving the learners the initiative to ask what something is can produce worthwhile language practice in class. A scene can be played, with the finger of a learner on the pause button and at the sight of anything interesting any member of the class can ask for the film to be halted. The class members can then ask the teacher for the meanings of the things which they can see. A further development of this technique as one of the ways of promoting discussion amongst the learners is given in the next chapter.

5 Transfer activities, discussion, and project work

5.1 Introduction

The earlier chapters in this book have been concerned with preparing for, and using, a video film in class. Two important aspects of the power of the medium have been referred to throughout: its richness as a resource material; and the stimulating and motivating effect of video on the learners. It is important that work with video should lead to some follow-up activities which are relevant to the learners' needs, and with which the learners can identify. There are two main justifications for this.

Firstly, as with any other language-learning text or source material, a video sequence is not studied just for its own sake. It should form part of an integrated learning programme, forming a link between different areas of language-learning experience.

The second reason concerns the nature of video presentations themselves. The vast majority of foreign language learners throughout the world have great experience of watching television for non-educational reasons. Reference was made in the opening chapter to the fact that in these contexts television tends to be a one-way medium. In an educational setting it is important that the relationship between viewer and television screen is changed. Several ways of creating some type of interaction have been described in preceding chapters. Transfer activities, based on the video, are a way of ensuring that the language learners relate to the pedagogical content of what they see.

The video presentation can be used in a variety of ways as the basis for further extended language practice. Some of these ways will use the video as a model, to be followed very closely. In other activities, the video material will serve as an input which triggers off language activities which reflect the learners' own interests and needs. The link with a classroom activity and the video may be just thematic; the follow-up activity may involve a completely different approach to using language.

5.2 Actual transfer

We can use the term 'actual transfer' to refer to activities which involve the students talking about themselves, their own circumstances and interests, or providing them with the chance to express their true opinions. A teaching sequence in the classroom moves directly from the video presentation into the realm of the learner's own life.

This can be done even at an elementary level. The necessary limitations here are the small amount of language at the learners' disposal and the probable need for the teacher to direct the activity. Nevertheless, valuable communicative practice can be achieved, which is the primary aim. The following example illustrates this, and shows how secondary benefits can be attained too. It is taken from the *Media Teaching Manual* for one of the early units of *Follow Me*. The video input is entertaining, and provides the learners with an accurate language model. The actual transfer, although related very closely to the video presentation, moves quickly away from the video to the learners' own interests.

STEP 1

Learners copy this viewing guide from the blackboard or overhead projector:

VIEWING GUIDE

Why do people like animals? Because			
	parrots	cats	dogs
they are friendly			
they are quiet			
they talk			

STEP 2 (video presentation)

Presenter:	Why do people like things? Let's see. English people like animals. Some people like dogs, because they're friendly. Some people prefer cats, because they're quiet. Some people like parrots, because they talk.
Parrot:	Hello.
	Pause button: learners tick off information.
	Frame release
Presenter:	Why do you like dogs?
Man with dog:	Because they're friendly.
Woman with cat:	I don't like dogs. I prefer cats.
Presenter:	Why do you prefer cats?
Woman with cat:	Because they're quiet. They don't make much noise.
Presenter:	Why do you like parrots?

57

Woman with parrot:	Because they talk.
Presenter:	That parrot doesn't talk.
Parrot:	Yes, I do!
	Pause button: learners check the information.

STEP 3

The teacher reviews with the class the information they have noted on their viewing guides. With a low-ability class, this may take some time. Notice that the viewing guide focuses on the key structures which the learners must master in order to express their likes at this level of language ability:
– I like X because it is + adjective
– I like Y because it + VP (verb phrase)
With a more advanced class, phrases such as 'I don't like dogs' and 'Why do you prefer cats?' can be picked up.

STEP 4

The teacher asks the learners to write down the name of any three things which they like. When this has been done, the teacher invites various learners to read them out.

Teacher:	What do you like?
Learner 1:	I like wine, reading, and the cinema.
Teacher:	What do you like?
Various learners:	I like wine / women / sport / bread / men / summer / flowers / sunshine . . .

The teacher-led activity can then be turned to small-group work. All the learners have heard the language model from the teacher 'What do you like?', and they have heard some of their colleagues practising 'I like + NP (noun phrase)'. As the learners do not know what has been written down by their colleagues, the group work – although elementary – is communicative within the classroom context.

During this activity, many learners may feel the need to write down lexical items in English which are outside their known vocabulary – such as scuba diving or carpentry. This should be seen as a bonus. By individualising the task in this small way, the learner greatly increases the commitment to the language objective. Furthermore, the colleagues in the class and group would hear something genuinely interesting, and learn something at the same time. A quick mime from the scuba diver usually makes clear what the activity is.

STEP 5

The teacher asks the learners to note down a reason why they like the things they have chosen. When this is done, the class work and group work proceed as in step 4. The target language structures will be practised, and may be extended to include examples such as 'because I enjoy it', or 'because it relaxes me'.

The above example is given in some detail because it illustrates the application of a principle which is valid at all levels of language learning. The personal concerns and opinions of the learners should be brought into the language-learning situation when possible. The note-taking exercise from *ESP Travel and Tourism* (in section 2.4) shows how the presentation of specialist information can lead to a job-related discussion among the learners. Some more examples of discussion techniques are given later on in this chapter.

The preparatory work which teachers need to carry out in order to set up a successful transfer situation becomes easier with practice; and this is no doubt true of most teaching tasks. The following interviews with young people concerning sport can be exploited in almost the same way as the examples from *Follow Me* given above. The transcript is from *Action-télé*.

— Philippe, qu'est-ce que vous faites au terrain de sport?
— Au terrain de sport nous faisons du football, du rugby et du cross.
— Aimez-vous le cross?
— Oui, j'aime le cross.
— Aimez-vous le rugby?
— Non, je n'aime pas le rugby.
— Vous avez beaucoup de devoirs le soir?
— Nous avons beaucoup de devoirs le soir, surtout certains jours de la semaine.
— Qu'est-ce que vous allez faire ce soir?
— Ce soir, j'irai me promener avec mon correspondant.

— Sandra, qu'est-ce que vous faites au terrain de sport?
— L'athlétisme, la gymnastique et la danse.
— Aimez-vous la danse?
— Oui, j'aime la danse.
— Aimez-vous la gymnastique?
— Non, je n'aime pas la gymnastique.
— Vous avez beaucoup de devoirs le soir?
— Ça dépend des jours.
— Qu'est-ce que vous allez faire ce soir?
— Je vais me promener avec ma correspondante.

5.3 Simulated transfer

The examples of actual transfer given above involve the learners as they actually are. If we disregard the necessary constraints of the language classroom, we can see that what the learners say is part of them. It is quite feasible that they would say the same things in a wide variety of different circumstances.

In simulated transfer we must recognise some dependency on context, setting and roles. For example, if the learners are asked to act out a scene in a shop, the topics are likely to be restricted to those which occur in normal dialogues between customers and shop assistants. One or more of the learners can act as customers and so speak for themselves. Other learners will have to act as shop assistants; this will normally involve simulating the role.

Simulated transfer retains its validity if the learners can identify with the proposed scene. The proposed role of the shop assistant is a necessary one to allow the other participants in the transfer activity to act themselves. The setting and the roles also determine much of the language which will be used. Cue cards, which help one of the learners to speak, should not be seen in this sense as restrictive, but rather as an *aide-mémoire* for the appropriate situation.

The following cue cards could be used with language learners at almost any level, to practise elementary structures or advanced social English, as a follow-up to a video sequence concerning hotel reservations.

One or more learners is required to take the role of hotel staff; the cue cards are then distributed to other learners.

Booking cards	*Complaining cards*
Book a quiet single room	Room is too small – has no view
Book a room with shower and view	Room has no telephone
Book a double room with a balcony	Room is too noisy
Book a single room and evening meal	Room has no hot water

The language produced by the learners will reflect both their own abilities, and the language they have seen presented to them in the video model.

Language courses which emphasise oral fluency equip the learner with the communicative ability to function in everyday situations. This emphasis on transactional language presupposes that a large amount of classroom time must be given over to stimulated transfer. As suggested in chapter 3, the video presentation of a communicative situation provides an especially valuable model and point of reference for the learners.

5.4 Games, quizzes, and contests

Games and puzzles exist in all cultures and languages, quite independently of any language-learning aims. In this sense, their use in the classroom provides a link with the real world; learners are given an opportunity to carry out an activity in the target language. These are activities similar to the ones which the learners carry out (or have carried out in the past) in their own language. An obvious reservation must be that many learners of languages do not, in fact, habitually play games or do puzzles in their native language. However, the commitment to these in a language-learning situation can be compared to the readiness to assume a strange role in a simulated transfer activity.

Once a game or similar activity is under way, then a different reality is valid in the classroom. A game has its own finite set of rules, for example, which control how it is played. Many language-teaching games can be used in any lesson, and most teachers have a store of games which they can draw on. The following example illustrates how a well-known game can be adapted to provide a thematic link with the teaching point in the video.

The game is a version of Noughts and Crosses (or Tic, Tac, Toe). It is a game for two players; they take turns to mark a nine-square grid with a cross or a circle, attempting to line three in a row. However, before making a mark on the grid the participant must successfully identify what is printed in the corresponding square in a parallel grid. This example is from *Partner* and should be read in German.

If somebody wants to put a mark in the top centre box, then the letters DB must be pronounced correctly in German. If the pronunciation is correct, then a cross or circle is marked on an empty grid. If the pronunciation is incorrect, then the player or team forfeits that go, and it is the other player's or team's turn.

S	DB	U
D	HH	BMW
BRD	P	DJH

Transfer activities, discussion, and project work

This little game provides a motivating follow-up to one of the teaching points presented on the video. It is clear that this game could also be used to follow any other language-teaching activity that may have been carried out in the class. This is to be welcomed, as it underlines the fact that the video presentation is an integrated part of the whole teaching and learning process.

This simple game, as presented above, can also be used with more advanced learners of German (or any other languages) by requiring them to produce more than just the letters themselves. An intermediate stage of ability might require the complete statement of what the abbreviation stands for; advanced learners might be asked that, as well as a short description in accurate German of what that represents. The Noughts and Crosses grid might then yield the following:

Letters	Meaning	Explanation (to be given in German)
S	S-bahn	a suburban railway line or station
DB	Deutsche Bundesbahn	the national rail network
U	U-bahn	an underground (metro) system
D	Damen	toilet sign
	or Deutschland	international car registration symbol
BRD	Bundesrepublik Deutschland	the continental name of the country
BMW	Bayerische Motor-Werke	the name of a car manufacturer
HH	Hansestadt Hamburg	the abbreviation used on cars registered in Hamburg
P	Parking	a sign indicating a parking facility
DJH	Deutsche Jugendherberge	a sign indicating a hostel belonging to the national touring organisation.

The letters in the original grid can, of course, be replaced by anything: numbers, dates, objects, lexical items for using in sentences correctly, cues for structure practice. The unifying factor in the lesson is the thematic link with the video presentation.

5.5 Language change in transfer situations

The examples in this chapter have shown how the type of transfer activity affects the language used by the learners. In some activities, the learners' language is modelled very closely on the video presentation; in others, the transfer activity leads the learners away from the language in the video presentation. Other factors can also affect the type of language which is to be produced by the learners. These factors include the mode in which the language is used (whether written or oral); the topic under discussion; the roles of the dialogue partners; and the setting for the dialogue.

Changing the medium in a follow-up activity

Most activities which follow a video presentation in class will be concerned with other media – for example, oral interaction, writing, or audio cassettes. Changing the medium also changes the nature of the language tasks for the learners. The following table shows different activities centred around the theme of weather forecasts. These may be taken from a specific language programme, or recorded from television broadcasts.

Language text	*Language activities*
TV weather forecast	Viewing comprehension Telling people about the weather Writing a postcard, mentioning the weather
Radio weather forecast	Listening comprehension Telling people about the weather
Newspaper weather forecast	Understanding diagrams Reading comprehension Telling people about the weather
Postcard / letter from friends on holiday mentioning the weather	Reading comprehension Telling people about the weather Reading about the weather to others aloud Writing a short reply
Project: learner-written weather forecast	Discussion about the weather Writing practice
Project: learner-made audio cassette with 'radio forecast'	Discussion about the weather Writing practice Oral practice

In this table the tasks for the learners move further away from the video presentation to project work. If video cameras are available, then the project work can also include video camera work (see chapters 8 and 9).

Changing the topic in a transfer activity

A video presentation of an interaction can often be followed by a transfer activity in which the topic is changed. The language functions being expressed can remain the same, but the change in topic will affect many other aspects of the communication – such as roles and lexis. The switch in topic can be suggested in many ways. One is to bring into the classroom authentic materials on which to base a simulated transfer activity arising from a video presentation. The following table illustrates this. The second column lists the features of a video presentation. The third and fourth columns show the changes that take place if the transfer activity is based on the use of a plane schedule and a restaurant menu.

Aspects of communication	Video presentation	Transfer activities	
authentic material	train schedule	plane schedule	restaurant menu
topic	train travel	plane travel	food and drink
setting	train station	airport or travel agent	restaurant
roles	desk clerk and traveller	desk clerk and traveller	waiter and diner
language function	asking for information about . . .		
notion	times and connections of trains	times and connections of planes	choices of food and drink

This table is valid irrespective of the language level of the learners. A practical application of this is that a video presentation at a relatively low level of language competence can be used as a reminder or basic model for a transfer activity at a much higher level. This can be particularly relevant when teaching a language for specific purposes. For example, the language of *fault identification* might be presented in a simple and structured way on video. In a subsequent transfer activity the learning group, such as software engineers, can have a similar discussion based on job-related materials.

Changing the setting in a transfer activity

Some examples in section 4.2 in the previous chapter drew attention to the appropriateness of language in different situations. One way of developing learners' oral skills in follow-up activities is to change the setting of the activities. A video presentation might show a group of tourists buying a quick meal in a self-service cafeteria. This can be the basis for a small role play which is carried out by the learners. As a subsequent follow-up activity, the same language functions can be carried out in a different setting. This could be a smart restaurant. In a self-service cafeteria, the dialogue is between customers and the staff putting the food on the racks, serving the drinks, and taking the money. The language areas covered might include asking about the food, ordering meals and drinks, and paying. In the restaurant setting, the language used to express these functions is quite different.

Changing the roles in transfer activities

Just as the setting can influence the choice of language, so can a change in one of the dialogue partners. An obvious example of this is illustrated by the data in section 4.3: the form of a straightforward question can change according to the person asked.

This type of language practice is particularly useful for advanced learners of a language who have had little chance to use their knowledge in social contexts. This applies to many learners in business, commerce and industry. Their knowledge and experience of using the target language is restricted to professional environments. Although they may be competent here, they lack fluency and communicative competence when put into social situations. One of the common reasons for this is the inability to match their language use with that of their interlocuters.

5.6   Discussion

Video is a particularly suitable medium for presenting language learners with material for discussion. This stems not only from the intrinsic merit of the living audio-visual presentation. It is also because of the adaptability of video tapes. Material from almost any source can be turned to advantage with the widest possible range of ability levels among the learners.

In chapter 2, suggestions were made on using visual cues for practice in note-taking. This type of activity can be carried out at the most elementary level, with carefully controlled language, whatever the actual language level of the film. Conversely, a sequence from a language-training video film made for elementary students can, nevertheless, stimulate advanced discussion amongst learners with that ability. In chapter 7 there are some suggestions for using specialist television programmes, in the native language, as a basis for project and discussion work in the target language. Such programmes are often made available on video cassette, or may be recorded (under certain conditions) from broadcasts.

As the range of topics for discussion is virtually limitless, this section concentrates on three aspects of this activity: preparation for discussion; leading a discussion; and learner-centred discussion.

Preparation for discussion

Most classroom discussions benefit from thorough preparation. Unless learners are very familiar with a discussion topic and/or are very articulate, an unprepared discussion can be disappointing. Learners are frustrated if they have not got the vocabulary available to express their ideas, and they are dispirited if the discussion leads nowhere.

If a video sequence is used as the stimulus for a subsequent discussion, then some form of note-taking is probably a pre-requisite. It is beyond the scope of this section to offer detailed guidelines on teaching language learners study skills; but the principles which are currently applied to other media can be applied in their turn to video in the classroom.

In chapter 2 there were some suggestions for structuring and guiding the note-taking of learners. In these examples the learners were asked to note down what they saw or heard. If learners need guidance in making notes on what they think and feel, the approach indicated below can be used. The checklist is taken from the pupils' notes to *Réalités Françaises*. The checklist should be completed after one or two viewings of a programme about justice, judges and legal penalties. It is intended to structure the learners' thoughts and approach to the subsequent discussion.

This example is given in detail as it illustrates three things. Firstly, the boxes with the statements can serve as a detailed viewing guide if prepared beforehand, to help some of the learners through the programme. Secondly, the boxes for the opinions will help the learners to clarify their thinking, and so contribute better to the discussion. Thirdly, the whole of the checklist serves as a very useful summary about the video presentation, and can be used in this way at a later date.

The main column of boxes with writing consists of a series of statements taken from the video presentation. The other three columns are provided for the learners to indicate their view of the statement: agreement; disagreement; or no opinion.

VIEWING GUIDE

Mettez, selon le cas, des croix dans les colonnes 'D'accord', 'Pas d'accord' ou 'Ne se prononce pas'. Essayez de vous familiariser avec les affirmations des jeunes gens avant de commencer l'exercice.

Affirmation	D'accord	Pas d'accord	Ne se prononce pas
Je ne pense pas que les erreurs judiciaires soient fréquentes.			

Affirmation	D'accord	Pas d'accord	Ne se prononce pas
Je n'accepte pas du tout la peine de mort.			
J'accepte la peine de mort dans certains cas.			
Je pense que des décisions de justice sont souvent des décisions politiques.			
Je trouve que les juges sont indépendants.			
Je pense que les juges sont trop âgés pour comprendre les jeunes délinquants.			
Les milieux défavorisés ne sont pas à l'origine de la délinquance juvénile.			
La délinquance juvénile n'existe pas dans les milieux favorisés sur le plan financier.			
Je fais confiance à la justice française.			
Le châtiment réussit à réhabiliter la plupart des délinquants.			
La prison réduit les possibilités de réhabilitation en rendant le prisonnier plus amer.			
Un ancien prisonnier a du mal à trouver un emploi à sa sortie de prison.			
Le taux de la criminalité est en hausse en France.			

Transfer activities, discussion, and project work

Leading a discussion

Teachers can successfully lead discussions without taking a leading part. The teachers' greater knowledge of language, familiarity with socio-cultural matters, and even access to teaching notes, mean that the learners' attention can be drawn to points of interest.

The following discussion points are based on a short sequence which contains only three lines of dialogue. It concerns a young couple looking for a new home on a typical English housing estate. Few non-English speaking countries have an approach to housing similar to that in Britain. Very few people rent houses or flats in comparison with many other countries. Almost half the population lives in houses owned by local government authorities; and most of the other half live in privately owned houses, being purchased with mortgages. The following notes are taken from the *Media Teaching Manual* produced for *Follow Me*:

Looking for a new home

VCR plays
Pause button: stop at very first view of housing estate

Discussion points: Housing estate – what sort of people live here? Houses – semi-detached, probably five rooms with a garage, and a garden front and back. Open-plan layout – no fences or hedges at the front, but probably at the back.

Frame release

Husband: This is the place. Let's go and look at some houses.
Wife: I don't know. I think we have to tell someone if we want to see the houses.

Pause button

Discussion points: Young couple – what do they work as? Who buys houses like this in Britain? (Probably young white-collar workers, teachers, company representatives.)

Frame release

Husband: All right. Let's go to the sales office.

Pause button: showing 'sales office' sign

Discussion points: Sales office – what services are offered by the builders or estate agents? (Probably arrangements for a mortgage – on new estates 90–95% of price – as well as help with legal aspects of buying a house.)

Examples such as this show that the discussion can vary in its profundity as well as in its language level. The insights into the relatively small deposit needed to buy a house in Britain (and the consequently relatively high mortgage loan) might set up a further discussion about consumer spending and saving habits in the UK. This would be particularly relevant for learners with an interest in financial affairs.

With certain groups of language learners, the teacher will not have a better background knowledge of the content matter than the students. This is particularly true in specialist language courses. This can be turned to great advantage in the language classroom. It offers a ready-made situation for genuine communication: the learners can tell the teacher something he or she does not know.

Learner-centred discussion

A discussion among language learners of a specialist topic with which they are familiar may mean that the teacher is left on the sidelines. This can be useful. The teacher can concentrate on guiding the discussion from a procedural point of view – asking for a summary, checking comprehension, bringing in another speaker. The content of the discussion can be left to the learners.

This is quite easy to achieve on language courses for specific purposes,

An interesting scene from Challenges *can stimulate questions from learners*

with a homogeneous group of well-qualified students. It is harder to achieve with general language courses.

One way is to give the learners the initiative for starting questions and discussions. If a video presentation is of interest to the learners, it is of course likely that they will want to know more information. One of the units in *Challenges* concerns the life of a young apprentice with a top London football club. In just a few minutes, a class of German adolescents asked the following questions:

About football:	Where is the Tottenham Hotspur ground?
	How many teams play in the top division?
	How much does a ticket to a match cost?
	Why are they all playing football at school?
About background:	Do all houses have so many chimneys?
	What sort of van is that?
About language:	Did he say 'you was asked . . .'?
	What does 'no, it ain't' mean?

These questions highlight some of the social differences between the learners and life in London. England is a country where many leisure activities are based at school; which has abundant resources of coal and chooses red for its post office vehicles; and has a regional dialect in the capital city.

Discussions without the teacher participating at all are a worthwhile language aim. Some suggestions for recording these with a video camera, and evaluating them, are given in chapter 8. An alternative way of having students work on their own is to set up project work.

5.7 Project work

Project work is a useful way to develop students' interests and extend their language practice. A wide range of classroom activities can lead to successful project work, and many projects can lead students into areas quite unrelated to the original stimulus material. The remarks in this section are therefore limited to projects which spring directly from the video presentation and which bring the learners back to the same video material at a later stage. Projects using a video camera are discussed in chapter 9.

Written summaries

Students can be asked to prepare, as a piece of co-operative work, written summaries of the video presentation. In general language courses this will often be in the form of a narrative. This writing practice is likely to prove an effective measure of competence in the use of tenses, syntax, and other written constructions. However, it is only of real value if the learners have a need for such writing in the target language.

With many specialist groups of learners this need is self-evident. Writing tasks for such groups might include describing processes, describing products and performance, formulating users' instructions, or drafting minutes of a meeting. These specific tasks will involve different but characteristic features of language associated with them.

Whatever the written material produced by the project group, the video tape can be replayed as a comprehension check. This in itself can provide a means for further language work. But it is perhaps most encouraging for the learners if the final video run-through takes place when the product material is substantially correct. This allows the learners to identify 'their' material with the professional pictures on the screen. An example similar to this is outlined in section 6.4.

Scriptwriting a role play

The first part of this chapter followed up suggestions made in chapter 3 for developing classroom role plays from video presentations of dialogues. An extension of this is to ask the learners to script a role play. Scripting involves more than writing just the dialogue. Stage instructions must be written; roles must be allocated; characteristics of the *dramatis personae* must be decided on. This type of activity is particularly useful if a sound or video recording is going to be made (see chapters 6 and 9).

At first sight the writing out of dialogue which will be spoken seems a waste – an uncommunicative, time-consuming activity. But this is not true within the parameters of the project itself. Just as games and puzzles have their own reality, so too this type of project work provides learners with its own stimulation and goals to achieve.

Scriptwriting a cliff-hanger

Many dramatic narratives are presented in instalments, or can be broken in two by the class or the teacher to provide a cliff-hanger: what will happen next?

Preparing a script which speculates on the outcome of a story is in essence very similar to the task outlined above. The main difference is that there is an element of 'right' and 'wrong' involved.

When the script has been completed, the students can act it out. When the acting is finished, the video presentation can be continued. The students can see how their script matches up to the script on the original film. This can then lead to discussion about which script is the better: the video script or the learners' own.

5.8 Summary

Some of the examples in this chapter have been given in great detail. The purpose of this is to emphasise the place that video tapes have in the language-teaching/learning process. The video tapes are not an end in themselves. Showing them in class should not be treated as the final part of a language-teaching sequence. It is essential that there is adequate follow-up work after a video sequence.

In the same way, it is not advisable just to slot video into a teaching programme without any preparation or follow-up work. It is clear that for many teachers video materials are a supplement to the main course. This is a quite justifiable use of the video in class; but the video materials should relate to the rest of the class work and the learners' needs and interests.

6 Sound only, sound off, and sound over

6.1 Introduction

The soundtrack of video tapes can be used in a number of different ways to encourage language activities. Although it is not always explicitly stated, video is an audio-visual medium; the sound and the vision are separate components, though normally played together.

There are three main ways in which the soundtrack can be used. The first of these is to play a video tape, and take the sound away. Some examples of this technique have been given in earlier chapters. A second technique is to remove temporarily the visual element of a video tape presentation, leaving the sound only. A third method is to alter or replace the original soundtrack with one supplied by the teacher and/or learners. This audio dubbing is particularly easy on video recorders which have stereo sound. Rather than use the two-channel stereo as originally intended, the language teacher can treat the machine as one with two mono channels. Some short non-technical notes on this are given in section 6.5.

6.2 Sound off and vision on

Removing the sound from a video presentation leaves the learners with only the visual element to interpret. The suggestions given in sections 2.3 and 4.1 show how the visual element can be exploited for quite specific language-learning tasks. The visual information can be used in much more open-ended ways if the learners have the necessary sophistication or language competence.

In *Systems One* the teachers' notes recommend silent viewing as a way of arousing interest and provoking thought:

The unit is played through without the sound, and the students are asked to think about the behaviour of the characters. Apart from providing a short lead-in, this section is designed to focus attention on non-linguistic behaviour and to develop skills of anticipation. In the early units when the students are not so familiar with the characters, it is important that this section is used as an attempt to identify character types – e.g. does Barry look and act like a Marketing person? This should encourage the viewers to relate what they see to their own experience and situation.

73

It is clear that very many sequences taken from television or language-training films can be used in this way. It is not always necessary for the teacher to remove the sound. In popular thrillers and crime stories on television, for example, there is usually very little dialogue during the action sequences. The soundtrack consists mainly of squealing tyres, the noises of the chase, and exciting music. In some language-teaching programmes, these silent sequences – without dialogue – are part of the programme. The first story in *Comedy Time* makes extensive use of silent film, even copying the cinematic style of the early twenties. In *Switch On*, the mystery of Valley Forge, which is central to the story, is heightened by the apparently inexplicable actions carried out by Vlammski. A 75-second sequence in unit 4 offers a particularly good opportunity for practising the present progressive tense form with reference to present time. The usual meaning of this tense form is with reference to the future; to describe ongoing events the present progressive is limited to occasions when the action observed is unknown, or puzzles, intrigues, surprises or upsets the observer. These criteria are met in this sequence, as the viewer is meant not to be sure what Vlammski is doing. The normal tense form to talk about action seen on the screen – for example, cooking demonstrations and soccer commentaries – is the present simple.

This technique is taken even further in *Speak Easy*. This is a film for language-teaching purposes, produced in mime. Within the limits set by cross-cultural constraints, it can be used for teaching any language. It can also be used with learners with different levels of language ability, even within the same class. The following extract from the accompanying notes describes the actions seen, with a short note of the language functions which are acted out.

The doctor then wraps a blood-pressure cuff around the patient's left arm, and records his blood pressure. She removes the thermometer from his mouth, reads it and registers shock. Again he tries to read it but fails.	express shock
She applies her cold stethoscope to his back and chest. His sneeze blasts her ears through the stethoscope. She writes out a prescription, hands it to him, and gives instructions about the dosage before dismissing him.	instruct someone give permission
Fully dressed, he returns to the reception area and shows the prescription to the nurse. She gives him a card for another appointment. Just before leaving, he sneezes a final time. After he has left, the nurse sneezes.	instruct someone

Making silent sequences is an easy and rewarding classroom activity if a video camera is available; some further details are given in chapters 8 and 9.

Vlammski is involved in intrigue in Switch On

The hectic car chase in Comedy Time

The sound volume control, which needs to be operated to take the sound away, is normally found on the television set or monitor, and not on the video recorder.

6.3   Sound on and vision off

It can sometimes be useful to remove the visual element from a video presentation by turning the contrast and brightness controls on the television set to their darkest settings, which obscures the picture.

Listening to the soundtrack without seeing the picture emphasises the importance of the contribution of the visual element to understanding and context. In programmes which are conceived in purely auditory terms – for example, radio plays – this information is supplied in auditory terms as well. But it is evident from listening to the soundtrack only of video sequences that much is missing. Depending on what is heard but not seen, the process of reconstructing what is actually happening can be quite difficult. This can be tested at home by teachers using ordinary television broadcasts. Without the viewer knowing what is on the various television stations, the picture should be obscured on one channel, and then the television returned to a different channel. At home, this can be an entertaining family game. In the classroom, it can provide the stimulus for discussion work among the learners. A suggestion capitalising on this is given in the next section.

6.4   Video split

Many teaching materials which are designed to promote communicative activities rest upon the idea of an information gap. Some learners are in possession of certain knowledge or facts, other learners must use the target language to find out what this is.

'Video split' is the term used in *Active Viewing* for the application of this principle to video presentations. The class is divided into two groups. One group looks at the video film with the sound off and the vision on. The other group listens to the soundtrack only. For this exercise, separate viewing and listening rooms are necessary, as the viewing group must not hear the soundtrack. Beforehand, it is necessary to make a separate audio recording of the soundtrack on the video tape. The cable connections between a video recorder and an audio recording (for making sound recordings) are the same or similar to those between two audio recorders (see chapter 10).

The type of video sequence used for this activity should be chosen carefully. No more than five or six characters should have speaking parts as this makes identification of the roles difficult for the listening group.

The sequences should be full of action; short pieces of dialogue accompanied by a variety of sounds are particularly suitable. Very dramatic or humorous sequences, such as slapstick comedy, should be chosen.

After the separate listening and viewing of the split video, the groups are brought together and paired off: one listener with one viewer. The notes in *Active Viewing* say:

The pairs orally reconstruct the sequence, aided by their notes. This is perhaps the most important phase in the activity as there is an eagerness on both sides to seek enlightenment. Interaction is usually very concentrated. The teacher should keep a low profile but remain near enough to monitor and advise. The final phase [of this activity] is to show the whole group the video sequence with the sound.

Further analysis of the sequence is not recommended. This final uninterrupted run – which may be repeated if the learners request it – acts as confirmation of the group and pair work, as well as a concluding piece of entertainment.

6.5 Audio dubbing techniques

Audio dubbing implies altering the original soundtrack of a video film in some way. The soundtrack can be replaced by audio recordings made by the learners or the teacher. These alterations need not be permanent. An expensive or valuable tape recording (which includes both sound and vision) does not have to be sacrificed for one classroom activity.

The technique to be used depends on whether the video recorder has mono or stereo sound; most recorders have mono.

Aim	*With mono*	*With stereo*
to change soundtrack permanently	plug microphone into video recorder; new recording replaces original recording.	plug microphone into video recorder; new recording on *one* or *both* tracks replaces recording.
to change soundtrack temporarily	record learners on separate audio cassette; play audio tape at same time as relevant video tape, with video sound off.	record learners on track one; preserve original sound recording on video tape on track two. Track one can be used repeatedly.

Audio dubbing offers the teacher opportunities for making difficult films more accessible to students. Simplified commentaries, summaries of what has happened, or even spoken reminders of what to look and listen for, can all help learners who would otherwise find the presentation too difficult. Learners' recordings can also be played together with the visual component of the video film. When these are heard together, the learners have the sense of fulfilment offered by hearing themselves speak against a background of professional filming.

Providing a new commentary

A new commentary added to a film can have three main effects:

– making a difficult commentary easier to understand;
– raising the language level up to the ability of the learners;
– replacing a native-language commentary with one in the target language.

This work can be carried out in a large number of ways: by the learners working on a project, by the learners working with the teacher, or by the teacher working alone.

Many film sequences are of interest to young and old alike, and to learners with different levels of general education and language ability. For example, a scene in a bottling plant will have quite different commentaries if it is used for in-company training purposes and also as part of a young children's television show.

In the same way, language-teaching films may be made with strict language control. However, as suggested in earlier chapters, they may be used with learners whose ability is far higher. These learners can provide their own commentary on what they see.

This technique seems to have special relevance to learners of a foreign language for specific purposes. It is often difficult for language teachers to get good video materials in the target language concerned with subjects such as biochemistry, metallurgy, civic engineering, and the like. Yet it is quite likely that television documentaries on these subjects are broadcast on the national television network in the native language. These films can be shown to the specialist language-learning group who make notes in their native language on the content of the film. On a second showing, perhaps without sound, the learners rely on their own professional knowledge to understand what is happening. Working then in small groups, they work out commentaries to match the film, but of course in the target language. This technique is also useful in mixed-ability classes: different levels of commentary can accompany the same film.

Supplementary commentaries

Feature films can be difficult to follow if after confusing action there is also difficult dialogue. In many of the popular series on television, action-

packed scenes are followed by rapidly spoken dialogue. The main purpose
of this dialogue is to advance the plot quickly so that the viewer can relax
with more action. At the more difficult sections the original soundtrack
can be turned down slightly and a supplementary soundtrack can offer a
simplified account of what is happening. Technically, this is a little
complicated to achieve. An easy way is to record the video soundtrack on
to an audio cassette, with the supplementary commentary being spoken
through a microphone on to the same cassette via a mixing desk.
Although requiring more equipment, this preserves the original soundtrack on the video tape. If this is not important, the original soundtrack
can be blotted out at selected points, to be replaced by the supplementary
commentary.

This technique is particularly useful if there is a self-access facility for
the learners to use video tapes on their own. If the available stock of tapes
is too difficult in language terms for the learners, supplementary soundtracks can be used in addition to normal viewing guides and worksheets.

Interviews and role plays

Many interviews which are presented on television are not confined to the
studio only. During the interview, the camera often cuts away to exciting
scenes which illustrate aspects of the interviewee's life. For example, if
the interviewee is a famous explorer, there may be shots of the Brazilian
or Tasmanian forests; if an athlete, then shots of races run and cheering
crowds. Learners can watch these interviews and prepare their own dialogue to match the pictures. The learners' audio recordings can then be
played together with the original visual component of the video tape.
This provides highly motivating project work for learners; it can lead to
much pleasure and enjoyment for the learners to hear each other apparently speaking on film.

7 Using authentic broadcast materials

7.1 Introduction

Video recordings of programmes being broadcast over the air by television stations are known as 'off-air' recordings. Once on tape, these recordings can be used over and over again, in the same way as commercially produced video tapes.

The legal situation concerning the use of video for educational purposes (such as language teaching) can be confusing. It varies not only from country to country, but can also vary from programme to programme; there may also be variations concerning the length of time during which recordings can be used, or who makes the recordings. Most of the legal restraints concern copyright; it is essential to check on the local regulations before making and using off-air recordings. Broadcasting authorities often publish information about the copyright of specific programmes for the guidance of educational institutions.

The safest way to avoid infringing copyright, if you wish to use off-air material and are unclear about the position, is to contact the broadcasting company concerned. Permission may be given willingly for educational use in such cases, if the situation in which the material will be used is explained carefully. Manufacturers and their agents, often allow use of their television advertisements ('commercials') for teaching purposes, if asked permission.

Making off-air recordings is extremely easy, from a technical point of view. Most video recorders have clocks and timing devices which mean that an operator need not be present at the time of the recording. Some notes on how recordings are made are given in chapter 10.

The unauthorised copying and sale of feature films (made for the cinema) is illegal. However, it is worth remembering that a wide range of video tapes – films, cartoons, sports features and documentaries – is available for rental or hire. In most countries, what is available will be in the native language, with specialist shops catering for the languages of various minority groups. This is fine in cities such as London, where it is easy to buy video cassettes in Gujarati, Greek or Arabic. It is less easy to find suppliers of video tapes in a particular language that can be used expressly for language teaching.

7.2   The wealth of material

The notes given here offer some points towards ways of adapting authentic broadcast materials for use in the language classroom.

Television programmes differ from specially made language-teaching programmes in many ways. One of these is length. Drama and light entertainment programmes are commonly one, two or even three hours in length. In this respect, these programmes are quite unsuitable for use in the language classroom in the ways outlined in the previous chapters.

The language content of television programmes is often quite different from that in language programmes. The language of television reflects the language of the contemporary society from which the programmes come or in which they are based. There is no control of language in the applied linguistic sense of course design, although there may be constraints of other kinds, such as censorship.

Against these potential drawbacks must be set two great merits. The first of these is authenticity. Most language learners are quite familiar with television from their own domestic situation. The number of hours they spend watching domestic television is likely to far exceed the number of hours watching educational television. In this sense, off-air recordings present 'real' television, in the same way that magazine pictures, restaurant menus and bus timetables offer 'real' material compared with a printed textbook.

A second benefit of off-air recordings is the opportunity they give for teaching learners more than just language. Teaching with off-air recordings means that media studies can become part of the subject matter of the lesson. Language is an integral part of the communicative message carried by the medium of television.

For the purposes of this chapter, television programmes are divided into three broad categories. The first of these categories is entertainment. This includes drama of all kinds, light entertainment programmes, shows and musicals, and even sport. The unifying factor in this group is that in a domestic context these programmes are watched largely for purposes of entertainment and relaxation.

The second category concerns factual programmes – mainly discussions and documentaries. There can, of course, be no clear border line between entertaining programmes which offer facts, and factual programmes which are entertaining. In general terms, however, there is a clear difference in content between a political documentary on the one hand, and a variety nightclub show on the other. The factor that the programmes in this category have in common is that they inform the viewer with facts and opinions.

The common factor in the third category is not concerned with content. It is concerned with length. This category – 'shorties' – covers those items on television which are on the screen for only a short time; ranging, say, from ten seconds up to ten or fifteen minutes. This can include news programmes, weather forecasts, sports results, lottery results, advertisements, charity appeals, religious appeals, poetry readings – in fact, any item from the wide range of television which fulfils the criteria of lasting a short amount of time. These 'shorties' are discussed in more detail in section 7.5.

Language-teaching programmes, which have formed the subject of discussion in the earlier chapters, are themselves often broadcast by television stations. Permissible recordings of these provide an extremely cheap way of acquiring a resource which, otherwise, can be costly. Many language-teaching institutions seem to ignore these broadcasts as a resource which can be taped and kept for future use.

Using off-air recordings

All the practical suggestions given in this book for using video materials in class can be applied in some way or another to off-air recordings. Many of the techniques are not explicitly restated here. Many of the differences in application of the techniques will result from the inherent differences in the structure and style of television programmes. A further difficulty for teachers is that there is usually no transcript available for reference during preparatory work.

The rest of this chapter presents some ideas based on actual experience. They can be radically altered and extended to meet the needs of different learning groups, and be based on different television programmes.

7.3 Programmes made for entertainment

By definition, this type of programme will be watched by native speakers for entertainment and relaxation. It is likely that the type of programme which appeals to a language learner on domestic television might also appeal when seen in the target language. Watching television in a foreign language might also extend the learners' knowledge of what type of programmes are available. It seems unlikely, however, that a learner who intensely dislikes quiz masters and contestants in the native tongue will suddenly like them in another language.

Plays, poetry, and literature

In many language classes, literary works are used as texts for enjoyment and/or study. These can include thrillers, science-fiction stories, structured readers, great novels, plays, or magazine stories. The criteria which govern the selection of these items for use with a language class are many and varied. There may be national or regional constraints – for example, an agreed syllabus, or the availability of certain texts. There may be local factors – special knowledge of the teacher; particular interests of the learning group; a visit by a famous author. Whatever these criteria are, they may also be used to govern the choice of any dramatisations which may be available on television.

The medium of television is so attractive for most people that it may be used to introduce learners to types of literature which are new to them. One of the main drawbacks with this type of programme is length. It is difficult to exploit a one-hour detective story in a language class. One common method is to use it as one of the last stages for language work. For example, the class may read a thriller (written as a novel or as a play); the understanding of the language, the related study of the text and the like, may last several weeks. When the class have a clear insight into the content of the thriller, the television version can be shown. In this sense, the television film is being used for a purpose akin to its original purpose: to entertain. The reading of the text in class can be as in-depth preparatory work for viewing, which was outlined in chapter 2.

A similar use of feature films for entertainment is on intensive language courses. After two or three days of hard work, with evening activities devoted to language acquisition and practice, it can be a great benefit to everyone to relax yet maintain an English-speaking environment.

Humour

Humour can be a difficult, but rewarding, subject for the language classroom. There is always a sense of achievement in understanding one's first joke in a foreign language. Nevertheless, many aspects of humour – rooted in socio-cultural areas, slang usage, obscure contemporary references and so on – will remain inaccessible to all but the most advanced learners of another language.

The following notes are taken from a video viewing guide used with upper-intermediate/advanced learners of English; they were civil servants. The notes refer to the first twelve minutes of a half-hour comedy programme called *Yes Minister*. The humour in the programme lies in the conflicts between the masterful civil servant and his Minister, who is supposedly his political master.

Before showing the programme, or even issuing part A of the notes, a considerable amount of pre-teaching was necessary. Firstly, the scenario had to be explained – in the same way as the sentence above introduces the reader to it. Secondly, the nature of one type of British humour needed to be explained – this is covered in the second paragraph of the notes. Although the storyline is based loosely on a genuine industrial disaster, the actual story which unfolds in the half-hour has nothing to do with it. Furthermore, the humour rests on the interplay of characters, not on the semi-technical background. The third part of the pre-teaching involved explaining to the learners what was going to happen. Some key words were explained, and the content of the main scenes quickly summarised. This in no way detracts from the value or humour of the programme; a teacher presentation cannot rival the well-acted presentation on the screen. Rather, it reassures the less able members of the group that they can follow the plot. At this stage, part A of the viewing guide was read through, and then used by the learners as an *aide-mémoire* during the viewing.

VIEWING GUIDE

> A This episode involves the Minister and his civil servants in a discussion about producing a chemical at a British plant in Northern England.
> The story is black comedy, based on the Seveso gas escape in Italy.
> Enjoy the opening part of the programme. Notice:
> - the Scottish accent of the Director of British Chemicals
> - the classical education of the civil servant
> - the party loyalty of the lady MP (Member of Parliament)

Five or six minutes were then viewed for enjoyment. During the subsequent pause, the learners were able to make comments or ask questions.

The next part of the programme happens to include an amusing distinction between 'suppressed' (a totalitarian action) and 'not published' (a democratic decision). Part B allowed for a small amount of note-taking.

> B The civil servant tells the Minister that there is a difference between *suppress* and *not publish* a report.
> Note the difference:
>
> | suppress | not publish |
> |----------|-------------|
> | | |

After this part, the storyline was simple to follow, and there were several minutes of enjoyment. The closing sequence under discussion shows the Minister making notes on what the civil servant tells him about disregarding a report. This includes discrediting the author, refusing to release the report in the public interest, leaking parts of the report unofficially, and so on. The tempo of the dialogue in the film slows down somewhat, apparently to allow the Minister to take notes. In class, the pause button can slow the film down even more, allowing the learners to make their notes on the third part of the viewing guide.

C   The civil servant tells the Minister that there are four stages in disregarding a report. The Minister takes notes. Take notes yourself ...

	useful vocabulary
Stage 1	to discredit
	credibility
	public interest
	security
Stage 2	reliability
	to leak
	press leak
	unofficial
Stage 3	off the record
	short term
Stage 4	long term
	....

The second half of the programme was viewed at a later date. The emphasis on language activity and enjoyment was reversed. That is to say, the pre-teaching ensured that the climax and denouement in the film could be enjoyed without specific language work.

To prepare these notes, the teacher had to see the film several times beforehand; but no transcript was necessary or available. This type of programme, with worksheets, and possibly a supplementary sound commentary, is well-suited as resource material in self-access systems.

7.4 Documentaries and discussions

The thematic content of documentaries and discussions dictates the extent to which they are used with any particular learning group. They are particularly useful, of course, for introducing the life and culture of the speakers of the target language to the language learners.

There are many television programmes which have a magazine format, and which are aimed at specific groups of the population. For example, morning and early afternoon programmes aimed at people at home, doing domestic tasks; or designed to appeal to a specific age group (adolescents or senior citizens, for example); or which concentrate on particular activities (gardening or painting). Within these programmes there are often short self-contained sections, dealing with one specific aspect of the topic. In that respect, parts of documentaries and discussion programmes can be treated as 'shorties' – see section 7.5. Generally speaking, the suggestions made in chapters 5 and 6 should be applied to documentary and discussion programmes.

7.5 'Shorties'

The reason for using length as the main criterion for grouping a diverse range of television programmes together is directly related to language. Time on television is an expensive commodity. The short, self-contained items on television have a particular message to communicate to the viewer – and must do so as economically as possible. Effective communication is achieved through the careful choice of visual materials, background noises, and language. 'Shorties' provide learners with excellent models of the target language being used for specific communicative purposes.

As with other off-air recordings, the techniques outlined in this book can be applied to 'shorties'. In section 5.5, different aspects of the classroom exploitation of weather forecasts are examined. Some television 'shorties' have a particular format – for example, sports results and news bulletins. For these, general viewing guides can be prepared in advance and used repeatedly. The guide can list the topic areas which are likely to be mentioned; at an elementary level the students can tick off the ones which are in fact mentioned. At a more advanced level, they can make notes on the content of the items.

The suggestions given below concentrate on advertisements. The first approach is concerned with the analysis of the language used in advertisements. This type of language analysis serves several purposes. On one level, it shows how certain language features are used for particular communicative functions. This approach can be used for initial teaching, but perhaps more commonly for remedial teaching. Another approach is to use the language in advertisements as a model for language work to be carried out by the learners. As a part of project work, learners can transfer from the original advertisement to ones which they record themselves on audio or video tape. Some further details about this are given in the following chapter.

This leads directly to a further consideration. Studying the language of television advertisements (or indeed any television programme) leads to a greater awareness of the role of television as a medium of communication in society today.

Language analysis

The main aim of television advertisements is to persuade the viewer to buy the product. To do this, information is given about the product, and there is a clear message that the viewer should buy. The following is a complete text of an advertisement presented by the owner of a leisure tours business:

Hello. This Skytrain brochure says I'm back in the holiday business. Ring 200 0 200 for my brochure.

In this short text there are two features which are characteristic of advertisements. The simple present is used in the product description: 'This Skytrain brochure says . . .' This is followed by an imperative, urging the viewer to take some action.

Use of the imperative is illustrated in the following transcript of an advertisement for detergent. The imperatives are in italics, as are the examples of the simple present which relate to the product description:

Trust today's Surf Automatic, and *get on* doing the things every mother does – and some of the things you want to do. Because today's Surf Automatic *gives* you Square Deal value. And with its easy rinse formula it just *gets* the dirt out, and then *gets* itself out – leaving everything fresh and clean every time.

Another very common feature in advertisements is the verbless statement. These say something about the product or are used to conjure up a particular image. Verbless statements form a large part of the following text of an advertisement for electric storage heaters:

Nice to wake up in the warm. Electric. With slim-line storage heaters. If you're putting in heating, a slim-line heater system runs on less than half-price electric. With Economy 7 over-night electricity. With today's fuel prices slim-line storage heaters can well cost you less to run than a boiler and radiators. Slim-line heating and a tankful of hot water. (cut to family scene in warm room) 'Hey, how did you get here?' Slim-line storage heaters – the boiler beaters.

Using authentic broadcast materials

This text also contains some other interesting items, such as the use of the 'if' clause and the word 'electric'.

An analysis of a large number of advertisements shows that two other tense forms are also frequently used in English: the present perfect; and the 'will' future. The following is the text from a made-up advertisement for a chocolate bar.

verbless statements:	The new, exciting, Crunchy-Wunchy flavour bar – with extra nuts and chocolate!
simple present:	It *tastes* delicious – it's so filling.
present perfect:	*Have* you *tried* the Crunchy-Wunchy flavour bar?
'will' future:	You'*ll love* it!
imperative:	*Try* some today – *buy* Crunchy-Wunchy!

This mini model of functional English at work can be copied by learners in their project work.

Media studies

Both the detergent and electricity advertisements quoted above communicate their message with more than just words. In each there are suitable visual images, which highlight in some way the merits of the product. The spoken message is also reinforced with captions.

An analysis of the language and the visual imagery is a useful part of a media studies course, or a worthwhile part of the general education of language learners.

Making spoof advertisements is usually an enjoyable task for all concerned. To be successful requires an insight into the way in which the target language can be used for communication. The following transcript of an advertisement for Guinness, an extremely well-known dark, bitter beer, shows that professional advertisers themselves draw on advertisements for inspiration. This advertisement is a parody of a popular genre, in which consumers are asked to choose between two products – and not surprisingly choose the product of the advertiser. Although the sequence lasts only forty seconds, there is a wealth of language and visual material. The scene is a crowded, friendly pub with the interviewer (John) and interviewee (Derek) at the bar.

This type of script, and the one quoted in section 6.2 from *Speak Easy*, can serve as models for learners who are preparing their own project camera work. These examples are relevant to chapter 9.

Time (seconds)	Spoken information		Visual information
0"			*Caption: The Guinnless Test*
	John:	Hi. One of the major causes of Guinnlessness	*John speaks to viewers.*
5"		is that many honestly believe that they wouldn't enjoy a Guinness.	*Derek gives ineffectual wave to viewers.*
			Barman nods in agreement.
	John:	Now, Derek, you are one of these people . . .	*Still talking to viewers, not to Derek.*
10"	Derek:	I am, John.	
	John:	. . . and you're going to help us with a little experiment, OK? Now, only one of these two pints here is a Guinness, but – we're not going to	*Cut to two pints. Pint A is pale – obviously not Guinness; pint B is Guinness – a black beer.*
15"		tell you which is which! OK? Good luck!	
20"			*Derek sips from pint A.*
	Derek:	Yep. Nice good pint.	
	John:	OK – the other one	*John speaks to viewers knowingly. Derek drinks from pint B.*
25"			*John gives knowing look to viewers.*
	Derek:	Aaah! That's	
30"		smoother. Beautifully bitter.	
	John:	Yes. So you prefer the taste of pint B.	*More knowing looks to viewers.*
	Derek:	Oh, definitely. Much creamier.	
35"	John:	OK – let's see which one you've chosen, shall we?	*John removes B cover to reveal Draught Guinness pump.*
	Loud gasps.		
40"	Derek:	Guinness! Amazing!	*John gives last knowing look to viewers.*

7.6 Summary

Television broadcasts are a major medium of entertainment and information for the vast majority of language learners. Their expectations of, and relationship to, television material are quite different from what is usually expected from educational television materials. The earlier chapters in this book have concentrated on ways of involving the learner with material presented on the television screen. The main aim of this chapter has been to highlight how the wealth of material in authentic broadcasts can usefully be adapted for the language classroom.

8 First steps with a video camera

8.1 Introduction

Working with a video camera in class offers both the learners and the teacher many possibilities for creative language work. But for many teachers the results of video camera work are disappointing. A combination of technical, organisational and psychological problems seem to combine to render hard work and endeavour pointless.

The main aim of this chapter is to outline a simple first approach to using a camera, which requires no previous experience, and very little technical knowledge. Teachers can follow the step-by-step techniques to instruct themselves; teacher trainers might like to follow the outlines given with their own groups of teachers.

Psychological problems

For teachers, these stem directly from a lack of experience of working with video equipment. The non-technically minded may lack confidence in using the hardware. Others may be uncertain about what projects can usefully be filmed in class, and how they should be evaluated.

Many language learners experience camera shyness, and may be slightly overawed by the equipment. Furthermore, lack of confidence from the teacher can engender in the learners a lack of conviction about the value of the video project.

These problems are most easily overcome if the first experiences with a video camera lead to success.

Technical problems and equipment

In the initial stages of camera work four main problem areas can cause difficulty:
– the quality of the soundtrack;
– the quality of the lighting;
– movement of the camera (from side to side; nearer to and further from the subject);
– changing scenes.
The aim of the suggestions in this chapter is to minimise these problems

as far as possible. The only equipment required is a video camera and a microphone (with a video recorder and television monitor).

This book is not a technical manual. The only technical knowledge required is the ability to follow the (simple) operating instructions that go with the camera and video recorder, and to understand this text. A basic explanation of how the hardware functions is given in chapter 10. At the end of this chapter are some hints on composition and an explanation of some of the terminology used in video film production.

Organisational problems

Organisational problems can be most frustrating for a teacher, especially when it is outside the competence of the teacher to be able to solve them. This concerns such things as the need to book special rooms in a teaching institute, the fact that video equipment is locked away, the lack of video tapes for recording, and so on. These problems are real and unfortunate; the solution to them usually lies in the institutions. However, successful work with a camera can arouse the enthusiasm of staff and learners alike, which may, in a small way, contribute to the solution of the institutional problems.

Four basic steps

The steps suggested in this chapter move from the simple to the more complex.

Step 1: A talking head – one person talks to the camera for a few minutes.

Step 2: Dialogues – two or three people are filmed talking together.

Step 3: Group discussions – a larger group of people are filmed in discussion.

Step 4: Project work – a freer use of video facilities.

Most of the material in this chapter is concerned with the actual procedures involved in making the video films. Chapter 9 offers some guidelines for making and exploiting the films that have been made. To a large extent, these notes refer back to the suggestions made in the earlier chapters of this book.

8.2   A talking head

A talking head refers to the type of television sequence in which one person speaks to the camera. To record such a sequence requires the minimum in many respects: preparation, expertise, time and stress.

This first step is deliberately simple to encourage success. Yet the simplicity of the technique does not detract from its validity as a worthwhile exercise. The talking head is used as a fundamental part of professional television presentations by broadcasting authorities throughout the world. For the novice using a video camera, filming a talking head minimises technical problems.

Setting up the equipment

The equipment should be set up in accordance with the manufacturer's instructions. A general schema is given in chapter 10. There is no need for the video recording equipment to disrupt the classroom. As figure 1 shows, the video camera, recorder and television screen can be conveniently located in a back or side corner of the classroom.

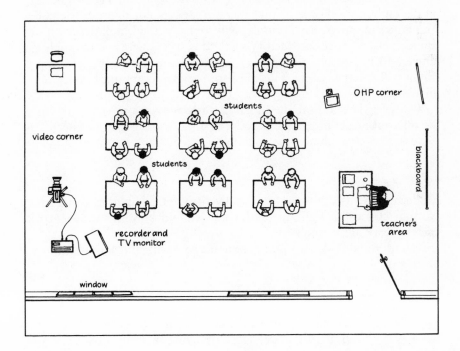

Figure 1

The camera should be set up four or five metres away from the table and chair to be used by the speaker. Use a tripod to set the camera at or just above eye-level height of the seated speaker. If no tripod is available, the camera should be held at the same height; this will probably involve the camera operator sitting or kneeling.

Sound

Many modern video cameras, whether colour or black-and-white, have built-in microphones. If there is a built-in microphone, use it at this stage. If there is no built-in microphone, place the microphone to be used on the table in front of the speaker and connect it to the video equipment according to instructions. The sound level should be tested before filming commences. Record a short sequence (which will be erased later) and play it back, checking the sound level. This can be done subjectively – just by listening; or by reading the sound level control dials. Many recorders and cameras have automatic sound level controls. During recording, it is likely that the sound control on the television set should be turned off or down to the minimum.

This is the simplest way of setting up a sound system. If a microphone is on the table, care should be taken by the speaker not to touch the table. Any finger tappings, for example, will sound as loud, dull thuds on the soundtrack. A more satisfactory method is to suspend the microphone above and in front of the speaker's face. This can be done by using a simple hook in the ceiling. There is also special microphone boom equipment available.

Whatever the solution, the sound at this stage remains constant. Once the microphone is in place correctly, and the correct level has been set, there is no need to change the sound.

Lighting

Modern cameras adjust automatically to different lighting conditions. Normal classroom lighting or daylight should be quite sufficient for camera work at this stage.

As with the sound, the lighting remains constant, and should cause no problems.

Camera work

Apart from switching the camera on and off, only one aspect of camera work is involved at this stage. This is moving in from a distance to a close-up.

Two camera controls need to be operated: focus and zoom. The first thing to do is to experiment with the focus control. The image seen through the camera, or on the television monitor if the system is so linked up, can easily be blurred or sharply defined by a simple movement of the hand.

The second thing to do is to experiment with the zoom lens. This has the effect of apparently rushing to and from the subject.

To prepare the camera for recording a talking head, follow the sequence 'Zoom In – Focus – Zoom Out.' Firstly, use the zoom control to close up on a head which fills the screen. In this close-up position use the focus control to produce a clear image. Lastly, use the zoom control to retreat away from the speaker; the speaker will apparently shrink into the distance, but remain in focus. The equipment is now set up and ready for recording.

Before starting on any specific language work the learners can be introduced to the camera. A lively way of doing this is to have the learners appear in quick succession, one after another in front of the camera. Each learner greets the camera, says who he or she is, and mentions one or two facts about themselves. If the learners have never seen themselves on a television screen before, this activity is a ready-made source of fun and excitement. Camera shyness can be quickly and easily overcome.

After this small beginning, both learners and teacher may be tempted to embark on an ambitious project immediately. Experience suggests it is more rewarding to move quickly but surely through a prepared series of steps.

The talk

Ask several learners to be prepared to give a small talk to the camera. This can be about any topic that can be explained in words alone. It is easier if the learners choose a subject which requires little or no preparation. These are likely to be topics of personal interest, such as the following:

my house and family – where I live, what my room looks like, my brothers and sisters / wife and children, and so on;
my job – where I work, what I do, why I like it, why I don't like it, and so on;
my favourite sport / my hobby / my holiday . . . and so on.

After sufficient learners have had practice at an impromptu talk about themselves, play back the tape to them for their own interest, without bothering about language-teaching points.

The next stage is to brief some learners to prepare a more formal presentation lasting two to four minutes. The topic can be agreed with the learners. It should not be too taxing, but the presentation should have an introduction, some content, and a conclusion. During this talk the camera operator should use the zoom control to move in slowly to a close-up of the speaker's head and shoulders.

The first time this activity is attempted there is no other guideline for the operator other than a clock. A novice camera operator is likely to be preoccupied with holding the zoom control; it is therefore useful to have a colleague standing behind the camera operator with a watch. When the required times are reached, the time keeper can tap the camera operator on the shoulder, to indicate the next move.

The scene starts with
a fairly long shot. This
shows the speaker, and
part of the table, with
the speaker's hands
resting on it (figure 2).

Figure 2

After twenty seconds,
the camera operator
zooms very slowly to a
medium close-up. This
position is held for
ninety seconds (figure
3).

Figure 3

The operator zooms
in more to give a close-
up, showing the
speaker's head and
shoulders (figure 4).

Figure 4

As the speaker comes to the climax of the presentation, the camera continues moving in very slowly to a big close-up of the head of the speaker (figure 5).

Figure 5

With experience, the camera operator does not need a time check. The cue when to move closer to the speaker will be given by the content of the speech itself. A useful exercise which looks at paralinguistic communication can be carried out if recordings are analysed and compared concerning the success with which the camera movements are allied to the spoken word.

Some suggestions for evaluating the recording are given in section 8.6.

8.3 Dialogues

Making a recording of a dialogue between two or three people is essentially the same as recording a talking head. The main difference lies in the way in which the camera is operated. There may be incidental differences concerning the sound, lighting and so on, depending on the nature of the dialogue.

Sound

It is possible to record a dialogue between two or three people using the built-in microphone on the camera. Better results will be obtained, however, if a separate microphone is used. With more than one speaker, a stereo microphone or omni-directional microphone is preferable to a mono microphone. The microphone can be placed on the table, but for preference should be dangled overhead (from a hook in the ceiling, or on the microphone boom).

Lighting

Lighting should remain constant at this stage.

Camera work

Filming two or three people involves taking the first step towards creative camera work. The technique of slowly moving in (as with a talking head) can be used, but the camera operator must also slowly move out. It is usual to end a sequence involving several people with a medium-to-long shot showing all the participants. More importantly, the camera operator must move the camera from side to side. This is necessary to concentrate on one of the participants at any one time.

It must be noted that concentrating on one participant does not mean always trying to film the person speaking. The microphone will pick up the sound all the time. This means that there will always be a voice-over, speaking the words, even if the speaker is not seen. It is often far more important to see the reactions of the listeners. The use of this technique can be seen daily in television news interviews.

Moving the camera from side to side in a controlled fashion is easy if it is mounted on a tripod. A locking nut, used to hold the camera in a fixed position, is loosened to give manœuvrability.

First-time users of a camera may experience difficulty in filling the screen in a balanced and aesthetic way. There are two main problem areas.

The first concerns moving from a close-up of one speaker in a group to another person in the group – also in close-up. If the camera is moved sideways – say left to right – from the close-up in figure 6 to the close-up in figure 7, the result on the screen can be disconcerting to the viewer.

Figure 6   Figure 7

This is because all the visual information that the camera picks up is also in close-up, and is apparently moving, sideways, yet this information is not really the focus of the viewers' attention.

It is far easier on the eye if the move is made in the following steps:
– from the close-up, zoom out until the person that the camera is going to

move to comes into the picture; this may require a slight movement of the camera to the right (in this example);
— start or continue moving the camera to the right, drawing the viewers' attention to the new person;
— zoom in on the new person, losing the first person out of the picture on the left; there may be a need for more camera movement to the right;
— hold the close-up.
This results in an apparently natural switch of attention from one person to another.

The second problem occurs with medium and long shots of a talking head or small group. At a distance, the shot is well balanced, but in close-up, the heads of the participants tend to disappear at the top of the screen. The reverse of this can also happen. The people being filmed are part of a well-balanced screen in close-up; as the camera retreats they appear to occupy only the lower portion of the screen, leaving vast expanses of emptiness above their heads.

Filming a pair is easily done with only minimal rearrangement of the classroom furniture

The solution in both cases is to use a small amount of tilt. On a tripod, this is controlled by a locking nut similar to the one which controls the movement from side to side. Tilt means pointing the camera more towards the floor or more towards the ceiling. Only a very small amount is needed to compensate for the differences mentioned above.

The emphasis above has been on slow, well-controlled movement. A common mistake is to swing the camera in all directions, zooming in and out — which can be great fun when intended, but is likely to induce seasickness in the viewers.

Extra visual material

There is often a need to show on the screen in close-up something which one of the speakers is holding or referring to. This may be a chart, for example. With one camera, which is static 5 metres away, it can be difficult to get a good view of the subject. One solution is to ignore the object actually being used, and to film a second copy, as shown in figure 8.

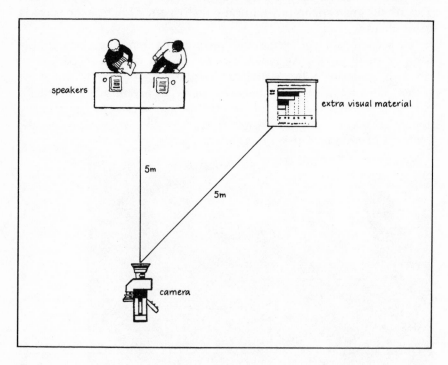

Figure 8

    The second object should be placed at the same distance from the camera, but out of view. When it is required, the camera can turn quickly to the object and zoom in on it. This provides a close-up of the object on the screen, and it is automatically in focus because the distance has been maintained. More skilful camera operators may prefer to have the object at an angle on the floor in front of them. This involves pointing the camera down quickly, and also adjusting the focus control.

    This device is particularly useful if one of the speakers is using something bright, such as an overhead projector. Turning the video camera on to an illuminated screen means that the amount of light entering the camera changes. Automatic cameras adjust, of course, but there is an awkward-looking transition period on the screen. This happens in reverse when the camera is moved from the bright surface back to the participants. A copy of the material being shown on the screen should be made, and filmed as above.

Benefits

The main benefits at this stage are:
- equipment is still static; it can be set up in advance and used again in the lesson;
- the technical know-how required is still elementary;
- the project itself is short: learners and teacher are more familiar with the technique; hostility, fears, giggling and shyness disappear;
- the subject matter is well within the learners' grasp, without extensive planning, rehearsal, or awkward silences.

8.4 Group discussions

A worthwhile group discussion amongst language learners requires thorough preparation. The topic must be agreed on, facts and opinions must be marshalled, the learners must be equipped with the necessary language to express themselves, and so on. Filming group discussions also requires more preparation than the two techniques outlined above. The step from filming one or two people to filming a larger group is deceptively large. The most likely problem areas concern the quality of the sound, and participants being masked by others in the foreground.

Sound

The human eye and ear can co-ordinate and focus on a particular sound source. This means that in discussions it is usually a simple matter to identify who is speaking. A microphone – at the technical level relevant here – is less sophisticated. When the sound which the microphone has recorded is played back, there are no clues about the direction of the sound. The microphone will differentiate, however, between speakers close to the microphone and speakers far away. If the recording levels suit people close to the microphone, people far away may sound too faint. If the recording levels are suitable for people far away, people close to the microphone boom.

Figure 9 shows the camera operator's eye view of a discussion, with an unsophisticated attempt at recording the sound. The microphone is in two sections: each a part of a stereo microphone. Although placed upon a piece of felt, it is susceptible to all the paper rustling, finger-nail tapping, and miscellaneous noises that are inevitable when a group of

Figure 9

people sit at a table. But in many circumstances, this is the best that can be achieved.

Lighting

Extra lighting might be needed to avoid shadows cast by the participants, or to illuminate other visual material.

Camera work

More use must be made of the camera, both in focusing, and moving in and out for close-ups. Notice that in figure 9 there is depth in the picture. This is preferable to having all the participants sitting in a straight line across the screen.

Benefits

Group discussions have the major benefit of involving more participants. A wider range of topics can be opened up by the group format, which in turn can lead to more valuable language practice. As the amount of preparation is greater, more responsibility for the project can be given to the learners.

At this stage, the learners can also be operating equipment themselves if they have not already been doing so. Once the teacher and/or the learners can operate the equipment satisfactorily at this level, more ambitious projects can be confidently attempted; some guidelines are given in the next chapter.

8.5 Hints on picture composition

Well-balanced images on the television screen are accepted as normal. Most viewers recognise the expertise which is there only when it goes wrong: an ill-balanced picture in a professionally produced television programme jars.

These hints on picture composition highlight some of the most common mistakes made by beginners. Making mistakes can, however, be a valuable experience. An 'incorrect' picture may convey, unintentionally, an image of violence, or quiet threat, or tenderness, for example. The beginner should try to discover what there is in the picture which is causing an effect that professionals use so well in film making.

A talking head

In section 8.3, reference was made to the possible need to tilt the camera to maintain proportions within the picture frame when moving into, or away from, a subject. Tilting has the effect of adjusting the amount of head room.

A head-and-shoulders close-up should leave head room above the top of the head. Figure 10 is better than figure 11.

Figure 10   *Figure 11*

A full-face close-up should not be isolated in a part of the screen. If necessary, the top of the head and the chin can be outside the frame. Figure 12 is better than figure 13.

Figure 12   *Figure 13*

In all the shots of a talking head, the eyes of the subject should be kept on the upper third of the frame.

If characters are sideways on to the camera, they should normally be placed so that they are looking across the screen. In figure 14, the man looking to the viewers' right is placed correctly on the left-hand side of the screen, rather than in the middle of the frame as in figure 15.

Figure 14   *Figure 15*

Groups

An important point when filming groups is to create the illusion of depth. This is illustrated by the seating arrangement given in section 8.4. Groups of people in project work should also be placed at different distances from the camera. The group scene in figure 16 is preferable to the one in figure 17.

Figure 16

Figure 17

A small group of people should not be isolated in the frame. In figure 18 the man and woman are standing too close together for the whole frame, and in figure 19 they are too far apart.

Figure 18

Figure 19

Other objects appear in camera range and should be taken account of. For comic or magical effect, various tricks can be used. Shots in which objects appear to grow out of the top of a person's head should be avoided. Figure 20 is better than figure 21.

Figure 20

Figure 21

8.6 Some useful terminology

Every specialist activity has its own jargon. The language of video production is functional, and quite accessible for the non-specialist.

Describing camera movements

Focus Up and De-focus	The subject is brought in and out of focus.
Zoom In and Zoom Out	The camera remains stationary, level and fixed in one direction; the zoom lens brings the subject nearer or further away.
Pan Right and Pan Left	The camera remains stationary and level, and is turned from right to left, or left to right.
Tilt Up and Tilt Down	The camera remains stationary and fixed in one direction and at one level and is tilted towards the ceiling or floor.
Crane Up and Crane Down	The camera remains stationary and fixed in one direction, and is moved to higher or lower positions on the tripod, while remaining level.
Track In and Track Out	The camera remains level and fixed in one direction, and is moved nearer to or further from the subject.
Crab Left and Crab Right	The camera is moved to the left or the right.

Describing camera shots

These descriptions refer to the image as seen on the screen. Because of the use of different lenses, the position of the camera in relation to the subject may be quite different.

The abbreviations given in the following table can be written into camera scripts in project work. The full phrases are normally used when discussing camera shots. The descriptions referring to parts of the body are further illustrated in figure 22.

BCU	Big Close-up; Face Shot	Part of the face or the head
CU	Close-up	Head and shoulders
MCU	Medium Close-up	Head, shoulders and chest
MS	Medium Shot	From head to waist
MLS	Medium Long Shot	From head to below knees
LS	Long Shot	Full-length figure
VLS	Very Long Shot	Whole set

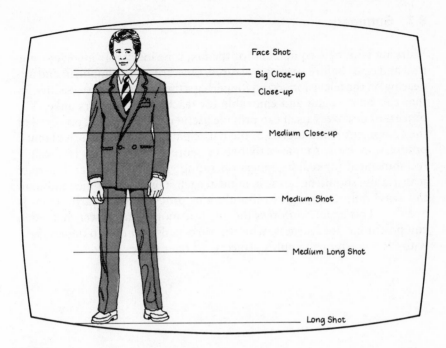

Face Shot

Big Close-up

Close-up

Medium Close-up

Medium Shot

Medium Long Shot

Long Shot

Figure 22

Describing scene changes

One camera offers little scope for sophisticated editing. Nevertheless, the changes between scenes can be varied. 'Cutting' is the term used for moving from scene to scene. Two successive scenes should be different in appearance, to help the viewers' visual comprehension. The differences can be in the distances involved between the viewer and different subjects; or in the angle from which one subject is viewed. If the camera cuts between different speaking characters, they should be looking at each other from opposite sides of the screen. If an elapse of time is to be indicated, then there can be a slight delay between the two scenes. This is referred to as 'Fade Out' and 'Fade In'. With one camera, this can be achieved by adjusting the lens controls so that the image darkens, making the subject invisible. The new scene can start with the darkened picture, more light then revealing the scene.

'FX' is a shorthand term used to refer to the special effects which may be required. Scope for visual FX is limited with one camera; some examples are given in the section on magical effects in chapter 9.

Sound FX can always be added to a video tape, as outlined in section 6.5.

8.7 Summary

Working with new equipment for the first time inevitably involves some trial and error before success is assured. Operating the equipment and appearing on the television screen for perhaps the first time are two activities that can be amusing and enjoyable for teacher and learners alike. The process of discovery itself can provide useful insights into the potential of the equipment – and indeed of the participants. Nevertheless, a planned progression from simple activities to more complex ones is strongly recommended for real beginners operating video equipment. A distinct realistic aim should be borne in mind at each stage of experimentation. In this way, failure through over-ambitious projects in the early stages is avoided. This again reinforces the intrinsic motivating power that video equipment has for learners, which in turn leads them on to undertake – with success – more complex projects at a later stage.

9 Projects with a video camera

9.1 Introduction

Once the teacher and/or learners can operate the video camera and equipment competently, a wide variety of stimulating projects can be undertaken. Whatever is recorded on video tape should reflect the interests and needs of the language learners – which means that the scope for themes and ideas is virtually limitless.

The learners should fully understand – and share a commitment to – the pedagogical aims that the teacher has in mind when a video camera is used. The types of activity that can be carried out can be broadly categorised in three groups:
- language-training video, which presents to the learners some aspects of communication in the target language;
- recordings of the learners, which allow them to see and hear themselves performing in the target language;
- video projects controlled by the learners, which offer the learners the opportunity of working together in the target language.

How the video recording will be used in the classroom depends on the type of activity; knowing what sort of classroom exploitation can take place is an integral part of the overall aim of undertaking the work with the camera.

9.2 Making language-training video

The video facilities can be used by the teacher to produce material which illustrates some aspect of communication in the target language. It is clear that for most teachers, working with one camera, there is no point in trying to emulate the professionally made language-training video materials referred to in the earlier chapters of this book. However, a teacher using a camera for work with his or her own class has the advantage of knowing in detail the needs and interests of the learners. The video filming can be tailormade to meet these requirements.

Most sequences recorded for language-training purposes are likely to present spoken language in its communicative setting – for example, short dialogues of people asking the way, making plans, and so on. The visual element of the screen presentation can also be used to emphasise paralinguistic features of language, as discussed in chapter 4. If video camera work can be carried out on location – in the country or area where the target language is spoken – socio-cultural, literary and contemporary themes can be brought to life in the classroom.

The remainder of this section considers four approaches to making language-training video; some notes on the classroom use of the video materials are given in section 9.5.

Functional sequences

Functional sequences offer learners language practice based on a model of language in a communicative setting. The sequences can be extremely short. Five seconds is enough to show a learner of language for business purposes how to greet a new business acquaintance. This will involve more than just words: a great deal of body language is also involved, depending on the culture. For example, in British English the full sentence of identification ('My name's John Smith') is said when the right hand is already extended; the elliptical sentence ('Pleased to meet you') usually occurs during the handshaking – but not after it.

Functional sequences can also be considerably longer, if a complex series of transactions is carried out.

Functional sequences are relevant to language learners at any level of language ability, and are applicable to general language courses and specialist language courses. The following broad categorisation of verbal communication is based on *The Threshold Level* by J. van Ek (1975):

Imparting and seeking factual information
– identifying and describing things; reporting on events and people; correcting information; asking for information and about things
Expressing and finding out intellectual attitudes
– expressing agreement and disagreement; accepting and declining offers and invitations; expressing and inquiring about possibility, incapability, obligation, certainty, permission
Expressing and finding out emotional attitudes
– expressing pleasure, dislike, surprise, hope, satisfaction, disappointment, fear, preference, gratitude, sympathy, wants and desires
Expressing moral attitudes
– expressing approval, appreciation, regret, indifference; apologising; granting forgiveness
Getting things done (suasion)
– requesting, inviting, or advising others to do something; suggesting a course of action; warning others; instructing or directing others
Socialising
– greeting, meeting and taking leave of people; introductions; attracting attention; formal and informal occasions – e.g. meals

Short sequences based on one of the categories above, or taken from similar catalogues of language exchanges, can usefully be used to supplement most language courses. However, the participants in the scenes must have a good standard of speech in the target language (if native speakers are not available), as the sequence is to be used as a language model. Making silent film avoids this possible problem.

Silent sequences: narrative

As silent sequences have no soundtrack, they are technically quite easy to make. There are no problems with microphones and leads; during filming, the camera operators and others out of shot can talk, give directions and instructions, check on things, and so on. On the other hand, the visual element of the video needs more careful consideration and control to make an effective silent sequence.

If the main aim of the sequence is to provide a vehicle for language practice, the teacher must be aware before filming of the various techniques for using the film with learners in class (see chapters 2 and 6). Narrative recall by the learners means that they will need the necessary vocabulary and structures. Speculation and interpretation will suggest modality and futurity as language points.

Making a silent sequence is also a suitable activity for a project run by learners; this is discussed in section 9.4.

Silent sequences: paralinguistic features

While the paralinguistic content of any video film can be exploited at any time, it can be useful to make silent sequences that concentrate on gestures and non-verbal signals. Groups of students can perform various mimes, which are shown to the whole class for interpretation and possibly copying. Comparison can be made between the gestures in the native language and gestures and signals in the target language.

The type of gestures and body language used will, of course, vary from culture to culture. The following list of ideas and feelings is taken from Leo Jones's *Notions in English* (1979):

OK	Beautiful girl!	Give me it!
Drink?	Sit down!	Take it easy!
Welcome home!	Snob!	Excellent!
Don't know.	Telephone!	Chatterbox!
Come here!	Triumph!	Be quiet!
Go away!	Goodbye!	Time to go!
Go straight on.	Stop!	Delicious!
Smell it.	Naughty!	Nasty!

Projects with a video camera

Yes!	disapproval	disgust
No!	scorn	Excuse me.
I'm angry.	surprise	sympathy
I can't look!	boredom	annoyance
Stupid!	liking	That hurts!
I beg you!	unhappiness	malicious amusement
Give me patience!	relief	

Sound can be combined with the video recording to add a further dimension to this technique; some suggestions for this are given in detail in *Active Viewing*; see also section 6.4.

Detailed examples of the type of language exercises that can be used with silent sequences are given in the printed materials which accompany *Speak Easy*, the video mime sketches for language learning.

Larger-scale projects

The assumption has been made in this chapter that only one camera is available. If more resources are available, more ambitious projects can be undertaken. These can range from more elaborate versions of the suggestions given above, to semi-professionally produced films.

Such projects can be used to produce video materials that meet the specific needs of a particular teaching situation. Many schools and colleges may not have expensive facilities themselves, but may be able to draw on an organisation with regional responsibility. This is the case in the state education service in Geneva, for example. Local teachers and advisers know the needs of the secondary school pupils learning English. One of these needs is for stimulating materials which concentrate on specific grammar points; another is for materials for cultural and literary studies. The local audio-visual aids unit met these needs by means of a large-scale project which involved making a film about Sir Walter Raleigh actually on location in the Tower of London. Here is an extract from the teacher's notes in *Reported Speech*.

SIR WALTER RALEIGH IN THE TOWER OF LONDON

Grammar
The main structure is the past perfect with only a few sentences in reported speech.
The whole film is built on the simple fact that if you describe a situation at a certain moment in the past you will naturally use the past perfect to explain it. In this respect a film is a very good medium since one can mix ideas and objects with perfect flexibility.
At this stage in the package, however, the presentation of grammatical structure is less important than the practice of language skills and the exposure of things past and present.

Style

The rhythm of the film is slow. We don't want the students to be fascinated by a sort of thriller; we want them to be able to see the walls, the towers, the ramparts, the lanes, etc.; we want them to understand what is said fairly accurately and in detail; we want them to have a good look at the room in which Sir Walter Raleigh spent so many years of his life – and to have a good look at the man himself. We were interested in the Tower as a prison, with its gloomy atmosphere.

Within the limits of local budgets, this type of production can be made without regard for the commercial constraints which often prevent established publishers from producing and distributing such materials.

9.3 Recording language learners

The suggestions made in chapter 8 for acquainting the teacher and learners with the video camera and equipment assumed that the learners would be filmed. In the first instance, this is to allow all concerned to overcome initial feelings of embarrassment or awe at appearing on the classroom television. In the longer term, the video camera can provide both teacher and learner with excellent feedback about language performance and competence; this is discussed in section 9.5.

If the aim of the video recording is to preserve the learner's performance for analysis and correction, then it is clear that the learner should be recorded carrying out a language activity that is relevant to his or her needs or interests. For example, a business executive may require a detailed analysis of presentational skills: language and gesture; visual aids used; manner and friendliness. At the other end of the learning scale, the video could be used in close-up to make clear to a learner why a particular sound or cluster is being articulated incorrectly.

The language that the learners use when they are recorded can, of course, be based on a language model supplied by another recorded video tape. The following list includes language activities that are common to a wide range of professions:

- making presentations: introducing oneself, one's company, or one's product;
- description: giving a detailed description of a new product's characteristics or potential; outlining a procedure or process;
- operating procedures: explaining how something works (from instructions and diagrams); demonstrating how something works;
- identifying faults: locating and/or explaining faults;
- interpreting charts and diagrams.

Existing video materials can provide a model for specialist use of language; the key structures can be highlighted by language analysis (see, for comparison, the analysis of the language of television advertisements in section 7.3). Using the model, the learners can then re-enact the scene, but adapting the content to meet their own specific learning requirements.

In the following extract from *ESP Engineering* attention could focus on the use of the 'will' future, the simple present, and 'if' clauses when describing processes; the speakers in this extract are discussing the assembly by a machine of a component for fluorescent lights:

Bill: Now the operator at this station *places* one of these brass tags in position, and *drops* it, merely *drops* it over the pin. It's *indexed* round again to a sensing station here.

John: Yes. Now that *sees* the tag. *If* there's no tag in place then the rivet machine *won't* cycle.

Bill: And *if* the air ejector *doesn't* work?

John: Ah, that's an important feature. Yes.

Bill: That's important. *If* the component's left on we *don't* want to start placing another one on, to cause problems –

John: A jam . . .

Bill: . . . on the automatic side of it. This *will* come down. Now *if* there's a component left on there, for example, that one, this *will* come down and it *makes* a micro switch. Signals from the cam bank . . .

By modelling their language on the above, and recording their performance with the video camera, learners can master the structures needed to discuss the components or machinery they use in their work. The camera records a transfer from the video model to a learner-centred version made in class (see chapter 5).

9.4   Video projects for language learners

The activities outlined in the previous two sections concentrated on presenting a language model and analysing learner performance. Learners can produce such programme themselves, in some circumstances. But a video project run by learners also offers other possibilities.

Making a video programme can be the end result of a project involving the language learners in a wide variety of activities. A script needs to be written; this can be commentary, dialogue – or just the instructions for a silent sequence. A shooting script also needs to be decided on. Various props will be needed – as well as the key actors, walk-on characters, camera operators, sound level controllers, and so on. If all these activities are carried out in the target language, the video project provides the means for language practice itself. Depending on the talents of the learners, and outside constraints such as timetabling and finance, video projects can be undertaken in any of the areas outlined already in this book. If the video presentation is to be the climax of the project (and not the starting point for more language work), more attention can be given to technical tricks and effects.

Magical effects

It is easy with video to make people or objects apparently disappear. During a sequence, the camera is switched off and the tape halted. The people and objects in the shot freeze; the person or object that is to disappear leaves the shot. When the camera and tape start again, the video recording carries on, recording the remaining participants. When the tape is replayed, the join between the two scenes is scarcely noticeable; the effect is that someone or something has suddenly disappeared.

The same techniques can be used to make people and things magically change place. For example, people's clothing – such as hats, scarves, coats and shoes – can magically hop from person to person. Mysterious objects can appear in several parts of the room.

Playing with the video in this way can be very entertaining for participants of all ages – from children to teacher trainers. With practice a variety of quizzes and games can be recorded: 'Spot the difference' contests; or memory tests, such as Kim's Game, in which something is removed from a tray of objects.

Some forethought is needed, as the recording on to the video tape will be made in a strict sequence, with the results appearing in the same sequence, if editing facilities are not available. However, the tape can always be rewound and used again to rerecord scenes that are not successful at the first attempt.

9.5 Evaluation

Evaluating video materials made with a class of learners should be an integral part of the language-teaching/learning process. Discussion of approaches to evaluation has been left to this stage as the first concern is the production of the materials. When a video camera is first used with a group, then anything goes. Learning to operate the controls, seeing images on the screen, understanding how the equipment works – these are time-consuming activities. However, it must soon be recognised that what is filmed must be worthwhile in educational terms.

Two general points are applicable to any video material made with a language-learning class. The first is that the evaluation of the material will reflect the aims of making the material. If there are no concrete learning aims, then there is no point in making the film anyway. The second point is that the suggestions given in this book – and many more – about using video films in class can also be applied to self-made films.

That is to say, viewing guides and note-taking cues can be developed for watching video materials made by the learners. This can be especially valuable if the video project has been carried out by a small group of learners, and the contents of the video film are unknown to the rest of the class; this is only one example – it is clear that the principle can be extended greatly.

More specifically, feedback and evaluation after filming should be characterised by two things. The feedback should be immediate; and the evaluation should be selective and sympathetic.

Immediacy is an elastic term when applied to filming; it means that learners should have the opportunity of seeing what has been filmed as soon as is practicable. Filming learners in discussion and then filing the tape away can arouse quite unfounded suspicions and even hostility among learners. They wonder what will happen to the tape; who will see their efforts; why they cannot see themselves. Of course, with a well-established class it is unlikely that such emotions will be aroused. But a guiding principle for people new to video is to let the learners see the results.

When language learners see themselves on the television screen, they are presented back to themselves as more than just language learners. What they say may be clearly heard; but also how they say it can be seen. They are communicating with the viewers in many ways, not all of which are intentional. For this reason the evaluation of video films must be selective and sympathetic.

Selectivity implies that criticisms should only be focused on things which merit attention. Sympathy implies that comment should be made in a friendly, constructive manner, and generally restricted to the areas under critical analysis.

Correcting learners

Video tapes can be used in the same way as audio tapes to capture the learners' language for analysis and correction. The most obvious features concern pronunciation, choice of lexis, and errors of syntax.

The audio-visual presentation on the video allows for the paralinguistic information accompanying the speech to be analysed as well. For example, the actions that accompany British English greetings can be analysed (see section 9.2).

A further area where paralinguistic information is important, but where cross-cultural factors prevent full communicative competence, concerns interruptions. There are many different ways of interrupting. The norm in one culture may be quite unacceptable or strange in another culture. And within a culture, the norms in semi-formal situations (such as business or academic meetings) may differ from those in a relaxed, social environment. Learners will often produce correct language which is inappropriate for the situation being shown on the video. In this case, exercises in appropriateness can be developed from the presentation. Examples of such exercises are given in chapter 4.

Teachers can apply to video presentations the same principles of error analysis and correction that they use in other situations. However, video is particularly suited for assessing fluency and communicative ability in specific situations. Detailed guidance on correcting learners is given in *Teacher Training Video Project: Dealing With Errors* by J. Revell et al. (1982).

10　A note on video hardware

10.1　Hardware, software, and accessories

This chapter is intended as an introduction to some of the technical aspects of video for people with no previous experience.

The term 'hardware' is used to refer to the machinery itself: the video recorder, the television set, and so on. 'Software' is what is needed to make the hardware function – in the case of a video recorder, the software is the video tape. Audio cassettes, computer floppy disks and pop records are examples of software. The accessories are the bits and pieces such as linking cables and leads. One could say: 'Provided that the software is available, and that the accessories are to hand, then everything in this book can be carried out with the following hardware:

1 video recorder 1 microphone
1 television set 1 video camera.'
1 audio recorder

What a video recorder does

Video recorders perform two main functions. They can record for later use programmes from a variety of sources; and they can transmit the programmes to a television set. More than one video recorder can be linked together to make copies of programmes.

Recording

Figure 23 shows how a video recorder is linked to an outside aerial and a normal television set.

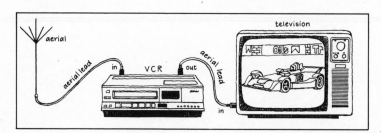

Figure 23

Television programmes can be recorded by the video in three ways:
– while viewers watch a programme on a TV channel, the programme is recorded on to the video recorder;
– while viewers watch a programme on a TV channel, the video recorder simultaneously records a programme from another TV channel;
– without the television being switched on, the video records a programme from a TV channel.
Household televisions have several selector switches or buttons, which are tuned to different channels. It is easy to retune any particular channel. Video recorders have a similar tuning system. To make the above recordings, the reception channels on the video recorder must be tuned in to television stations in exactly the same way as the channels on the television set. The mechanism by which the video recorder can record various programmes, regardless of what the viewer is doing, may vary slightly from machine to machine; but the facility is standard. Exact details and instructions accompany each machine.

The practical effect of this for language teachers is that a programme broadcast when the teaching institution is closed can nevertheless be recorded for later use. Recordings from a video camera can be made whenever the camera is operating.

Figure 24 shows schematically a video camera linked to a recorder. A television screen is not shown, as it is not necessary to make the recordings: a viewfinder on the camera itself shows (in miniature) what would be seen on a television screen, if connected. However, a television set can be linked to the recorder so that the recording can be watched as it is made. Using a televison set in this way is essential with cameras *without* a built-in viewfinder.

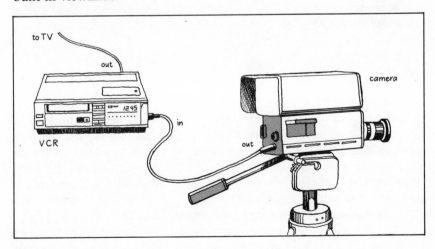

Figure 24

A note on video hardware

In certain circumstances, a video camera can be linked directly to a television screen, showing on the screen what the camera sees. This is useful, for example, in order to show an assembly outside a closed meeting room what is happening inside the room. This device is commonly used for religious and political meetings, as well as some academic lectures. This is shown in figure 25.

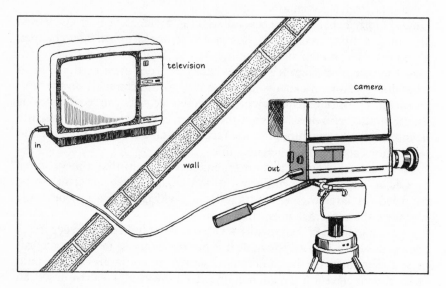

Figure 25

The leads and cables which are necessary to effect the above recordings are supplied with the equipment; making the right connections is also easy.

Playback

During the playback mode, a video recorder functions as a television broadcasting station. That is to say, it transmits its message to the television set. To receive the national broadcasting stations the television set must be tuned in. To receive the video programme, a channel on the television set must be tuned in to receive the broadcast from the video recorder. On many modern television sets, one channel is designated as particularly suitable for receiving video programmes. This should be used if it is so marked (although in fact any channel can be used).

When the television set is showing the material on the video tape, the television controls will function as normal. The video controls are only used to stop, start or rewind the tape.

Copying

With two or more video recorders, it is possible to make copies of video tapes. With the right accessories it does not matter – for copying purposes – what the two types of video recorders are. But as the next section shows, there are major differences between the different types of video recorders available, which can cause problems for the unwary. Making copies of video material may be illegal, or restricted by copyright laws. If necessary, permission to make copies should be sought (see section 7.1).

10.2 Types of video recorder

There are four major video systems available worldwide. The domestic market for video recorders is dominated by three systems, known as VHS, Betamax, and Video 2000. These systems are also common in teaching institutions. In many institutions, though rarely in households, there are also machines made to the U-matic system.

The U-matic machines are designed primarily for semi-professional use. For this reason, they are often found in institutions with video studio facilities, or with regional responsibility for visual aids.

All these machines use closed video cassettes; machines which use video tape on open spools are not discussed here; they are not frequently found in homes or teaching institutions.

For the purposes of language teaching as outlined in this book, all four systems offer high-quality technical performance. Any one machine is quite suitable; the only drawback is if one wants to use different machines. Each of the four systems has an entirely different design; the cassettes which are used on each system have different physical dimensions, and will not fit into a machine of another system. This lack of compatibility is expected to last for some time.

If a school or institution plans to purchase a video recorder, inquiries should be made about the availability of cassettes in that video format; the type of machine used by other institutions with whom there is liaison; and the recommendations of regional and national authorities. There is a further complication concerning television broadcast systems. France, the UK and the USA, for example, each use a different television standard.

10.3 Television broadcast standards

The technology which is used to broadcast television programmes is not the same in every country in the world. There are three main systems, or standards, although within any one country only one standard is used.

This has no effect on users of television and video recorders within a country. It may affect people who wish to use equipment purchased in one country in a different country; or who wish to send tapes to another country.

The differences discussed here are nothing to do with the video recorders and their incompatibility, outlined in section 10.2. For example a VHS recorder can be used to make a video tape recording in the UK; when the tape is played in France, a colour tape plays as a black-and-white tape. This is because the national television standard in France is based on different technology than in the UK.

The three main systems are known as PAL, SECAM, and NTSC. The first two are normally pronounced as words. The following table indicates the main users of each system.

PAL	*NTSC*	*SECAM*
Argentina	Canada	France
Australia	Japan	Greece
Bahrain	Mexico	Iraq
Hong Kong	USA	Saudi Arabia
Indonesia		USSR
Israel		Zimbabwe
Malaysia		
New Zealand		
Nigeria		
Pakistan		
Singapore		
South Africa		
Sudan		
Western Europe including UK		
(most countries unless		
listed under SECAM)		

10.4 Features of video recorders

The facilities on video recorders have not been designed for language-teaching purposes. They have been designed, in the main, to meet the supposed needs of the domestic television viewer and video user. For language teaching, the facilities can be divided broadly into three groups – the absolutely essential; the very useful; and the useful that can nevertheless be dispensed with if cost is an important factor.

Essential features

All video recorders have a stop-and-start button – otherwise they could not operate. They also have a rewind control, which winds the tape back to an earlier part of the sequence. With this control is also a fast-forward control, which winds a tape on to a later place.

Very useful features

These very useful features have been tacitly assumed in this book:

Pause button –   this stops the tape momentarily, allowing for an immediate re-start.

Freeze Frame –   this stops the tape in the same way as a pause button but retains a frozen picture on the screen. On some machines, there is a slight loss of sound when the tape is restarted after the pause button or freeze frame has been used. A technician may be able to adjust the machine; if this drawback is too noticeable, another machine should be purchased.

Picture search –   this allows the tape to be wound forwards or backwards at speed, with a fast-moving picture flashing across the screen. This is extremely useful for teachers' preparation: it allows scenes on video tapes to be located quickly and accurately.

Remote control –   remote control facilities may be linked to the video recorder by a cable; or they may use some infra-red technique. Remote control is extremely useful in classroom work, as the operator of the video recorder need not stand near the machine.

Larger counter digits – as the tape is wound forwards or backwards, so a counter increases or decreases. It can be useful to have a counter with large digits, so that they can be seen from across a classroom. However, there may be little choice available regarding this facility.

Slow motion facility – this slows down the action; normally the sound is lost.

As a rule of thumb, if a video recorder has remote control and picture search facilities, it will have enough other facilities built in to meet the needs of most language-teaching situations.

Useful features

Stereo sound –   this enables the use of two soundtracks, as outlined in chapter 6.

A note on video hardware

Double speed with sound – this facility allows tapes to be played at double speed with no loss of soundtrack. This is particularly useful for preparation with video tapes when most of the language content is in fact known.

Classroom exploitation of video recorder facilities

The techniques outlined in this book for using the video recorder in the classroom depend on the facilities available on the recorder. With a little practice it is quite easy to develop and invent different techniques, based on whatever the video recorder offers.

For example, speculation about character can be encouraged by removing the colour from a sequence. The double speed facility with sound can be used with learners to analyse how they listen for gist. The forward picture search can be used to initiate games such as Crime Witness: who can give an accurate account of what they have seen?

There is no complete catalogue of techniques for using video equipment in the classroom; with the inventiveness of teachers using video worldwide it is unlikely that there ever will be.

Postscript

This book has attempted to introduce teachers and teacher trainers to some general principles concerning the use of simple video equipment in the language classroom. Many readers will have recognised in the suggestions teaching techniques that they already use; this should be considered an advantage. Teaching with video equipment does not imply that an entirely new methodology should take over. Proven ideas and approaches should be adapted to make the most of the new technology.

For many readers, there will have been material here that is new, and, it is hoped, instructive. These insights into teaching with video should be related to the teacher's own professional experience and local conditions. With a little practice, teachers can develop their own techniques and language-learning materials.

A book of this sort has to be selective. There is little about teacher-training uses of video (although a great deal can be inferred from the examples given). Similarly, the book is restricted to simple video equipment: basically, a camera and video recorder. The teaching possibilities with video studios, mixing and editing facilities, permanent help from technical staff, and so on, are not discussed. Also omitted are references to the microchip, computers in education, teletext information services, etc. There is scarcely a limit to what new technology can offer the language learners of the future. However, the same approach to using these new media in language teaching must apply: the teacher should analyse what the technology can offer; apply sound pedagogical principles to that; and adapt and use the technology for his or her own specific language-teaching situation.

Bibliography A   Materials referred to in the text

The video materials and books referred to in the text are listed here in separate groups; the video materials are listed alphabetically by title.

Video materials

Action-télé, Thames Television, 1980. A beginners' course in French for children aged 10–13 years

Alles klar, BBC Television for Schools, 1982. Supplementary materials in German for children aged 13–16 years

The Bellcrest Story, BBC English by Radio and Television, 1973. An advanced course in business English for adults

Bid for Power, BBC English by Radio and Television, 1982. An intermediate course in business English for adults

Challenges, BBC English by Radio and Television, 1978. Supplementary course material in English at an advanced level for older children and young adults

Classroom Video: Functional Sequences, The British Council, 1982. Supplementary material in English at an elementary level for adults

Classroom Video: Viewing Comprehension, The British Council, 1982. Supplementary material in English at intermediate and advanced level for adults. N.B. A revised version of this is published as *Video English*, Macmillan, 1983

Comedy Time, BBC English by Radio and Television, 1982. Supplementary material in English at an elementary level for all ages

ESP Business, Nelson Filmscan, 1982. An advanced course in business English for adults

ESP Engineering, Nelson Filmscan, 1982. An advanced course in engineering English for adults

ESP Travel and Tourism, Nelson Filmscan, 1982. An advanced course in English in travel and tourism for adults

Follow Me, BBC English by Radio and Television, 1979. A course in elementary English for adults

It's Your Turn to Speak, Nelson Filmscan, 1982. A refresher course at an elementary level in British English and American English for adults

On We Go, BBC English by Radio and Television, 1972. A beginners' course in English for children aged 11–13 years

Partner, Thames Television, 1984. A beginners' course in German for children aged 11–13 years

Réalités Françaises, Thames Television, 1981. Supplementary materials in French at an advanced level for older children and young adults

Reported Speech, Service des Moyens Audio-visuels, Geneva, 1977.
  Supplementary materials in English at an intermediate level for children aged
  15–18 years
The Sadrina Project, BBC English by Radio and Television, 1979. A course in the
  language of tourism at an intermediate level for adults
Speak Easy, BBC English by Radio and Television, 1982. Supplementary material
  in mime for teaching any language with all age groups at any level
Switch On, Nelson Filmscan, 1982. A refresher course at an elementary level in
  American English for adults, designed for self-study or classroom work
Systems One, Language Training Services, 1982. An advanced course in business
  English for adults
We Mean Business, Armand Colin/Longman, Paris, 1983. Video material to
  supplement an existing course in elementary business English
Wie sagt man . . .?, Thames Television, 1980. Supplementary material at an
  intermediate level in German for school children aged 14–16 years
Yes Minister, BBC Television comedy series

Books

Gaderer, H. & Lonergan, J. (eds.), *Media Teaching Manual*, Verband
  Oesterreichischer Volkshochschulen, Vienna/Deutscher
  Volkshochschul-Verband, Frankfurt, 1980
Jones, L., *Notions in English*, Cambridge University Press, 1979
Lavery, M., *Active Viewing*, Pilgrim's Publications, Canterbury, 1981
Revell, J., et al., *Teacher Training Video Project: Dealing With Errors*, British
  Council, 1982
van Ek, J., *The Threshold Level*, Council of Europe, Strasbourg, 1975

Bibliography B   Further reading

The first three items listed are bibliographies, which give details of a great number of specialist articles and books concerning teaching with the media. The other items are listed alphabetically by author.

CILT – Centre for Information on Language Teaching and Research, 20 Carlton House Terrace, London SW1Y 5AP, UK. Specialised bibliography B13: *The Use of Radio, Television, Video and Films in Language Teaching*

ERIC Clearinghouse on Languages and Linguistics, 3520 Prospect Street, N.W., Washington, D.C.20007. Computer search and printout (449): *TV and Video Tapes in Second Language Learning*

Gazdar, Aban (ed.), *Fremdsprachenlernen mit Hörfunk und Fernsehen: eine Bibliographie ausgewählter Fachliteratur*, Internationales Zentralinstitut für das Jugend- und Bildungsfernsehen, Munich, 1979

Boczkowski, I., Lonergan, J., Topp, H. J., Weissling, H., *Handreichung für Kursleiter zum Medienverbund Englisch*, PAS DVV Frankfurt, 1979

British Journal of Language Teaching, Special Issue, 'The use of broadcast material in language teaching', vol. XVIII, no. 2/3, Winter 1980

Brumfit, C. (ed.), *Video Applications in Language Teaching*, Pergamon Press, Oxford, 1983

Dowmunt, T., *Video with Young People*, Inter-action Imprint, London, 1980

ELT Documents: 105 – *The Use of the Media in English Language Teaching*, The British Council, London, 1979

Gaderer, H., & Lonergan, J. (eds.), *Media Teaching Manual*, DVV Frankfurt/VOeV, Vienna, 1980

Geddes, M., & Sturtridge, G. (eds.), *Video in the Language Classroom*, Heinemann, London, 1982

Laver, J., & Hutcheson, S. (eds.), *Communication in Face to Face Interaction*, Penguin, Harmondsworth, 1972

Lonergan, J., 'Video recordings in language teaching', *Media in Education and Development*, vol. 15, no. 1, The British Council, 1982

Lonergan, J., 'The value of video activities for secondary school teachers', *Practical English Teacher*, June 1983

Northedge, A., *How to Study*, The Open University, Milton Keynes, 1978

Open University, *Learning from Television – a Study Package*, The Open University, Milton Keynes, 1981

Owen, D., & Dunton, M., *The Complete Handbook of Video*, Penguin, Harmondsworth, 1982

Rybak, S., *Learning Languages from the BBC*, BBC Education, London, 1980

UPLEGESS Contact, 'Spécial Vidéo', *Anales*, Bordeaux, 1983
van Ek, J., *Systems Development in Adult Language Learning: The Threshold Level*, Council of Europe, Strasbourg, 1975
Vogel, G., Weise, H., Fitzpatrick, A., Lonergan, J., 'Mediendidaktische Handreichungen: Follow Me', *Weiterbildung und Medien*, 2 (1979)
Watrelos, A. M., White, R., et al. *Teacher Training File*, Formavision, Paris, 1982
Wright, D., 'Role-play, simulations and video in TEFL: where are we now and where do we go from here?', *Perspectives in Academic Gaming and Simulation 5*, Kogan Page, London, 1980

Acknowledgements

The author and publishers are grateful to the following for permission to reproduce material:

BBC: extracts from *The Bellcrest Story* on pp. 17, 23, 35 and photo on p. 43; extract from *Alles klar* on p. 22; extracts from *Follow Me* on pp. 27, 36–7 and photos on pp. 12, 52; extract from *On We Go* on pp. 21–2; photos from *Challenges* on pp. 19, 69; photo from *Bid For Power* on p. 46; photo from *The Sadrina Project* on p. 44; photo from *Comedy Time* on p. 75; extract from *Speak Easy* on p. 74. Thames Television: extracts from *Action-télé* on pp. 13–14, 59; extract from *Partner* on p. 61; extract from *Réalités Françaises* on pp. 66–7; extract from *Wie sagt man . . .?* on pp. 17–18. Nelson Filmscan: extract from *ESP Business* on p. 42; extract from *ESP Engineering* on p. 114; extract from *ESP Travel and Tourism* on pp. 25–6; extract from *It's Your Turn to Speak* on pp. 38–9 and photo on p. 38; photos from *Switch On* on pp. 29, 75. The British Council: extracts from *Classroom Video: Functional Sequences* on pp. 33–4; extract from *Classroom Video: Viewing Comprehension* on p. 51. Service des Moyens Audio-visuels: extract from *Reported Speech* on pp. 112–13. VOeV/DVV: extracts from *Media Teaching Manual* on pp. 12–13, 14, 20–1, 26–7, 36–7, 57, 68. Guinness and Co. Ltd: transcript of advertisement on p. 89.

Photos on pp. 96–7, 98, 99, 103–5 by Cui Zhi Ming (Peking), courtesy of International House, London.
Drawings by Chris Evans and David Mostyn.

Index

Index

hardware, 118–24
humour, 83–5, 89

'if' clauses, 47, 52, 114
imperative, 87–8
interviews, 79; *see also* discussions
intonation, 33–6, 116
It's Your Turn to Speak, 33, 38–9,
   127

learner: learner-centred activities, 10,
   23, 28, 56, 69–70, 114–17; role of,
   6–7
lexis, 37, 55
literature, 82–3
lighting, 94, 97, 102

magical effects, 115
media studies, 88
Media Teaching Manual, 12–13, 14,
   20–1, 26–7, 36–7, 57, 68, 127
mime, 35, 73–7, 111–12; *see also*
   gestures
mono soundtrack, 77
multiple choice: closed set, 12–13;
   open set, 14

note-taking, 20–31; free, 28–9;
   guided, 24–8; sorting information,
   20–4
Notions in English, 111, 127
NTSC, television system, 122

off-air recordings, vii, 80–90:
   documentaries, 86; entertainment
   programmes, 82–5; 'shorties',
   86–9
On We Go, 21–2, 126

PAL, television system, 122
pan, camera technique, 106
paralinguistic features, 4, 10, 34,
   41–55, 73–6, 111–12, 113, 116
Partner, 61–2, 126
past continuous in English, 48
past perfect in English, 48
pause button, 26–7, 32, 123
predictive speech, 32, 36–9

present perfect: in English, 52; in
   German, 48
present simple in English 52, 87–8,
   114
project work, 56, 70–2, 109–17
pronouns, address forms, 54
prosodic features, 41–2

Réalités Françaises, 66–7, 126
register, 41, 45–7
repetition, 32–6; of gesture, 34–6; of
   intonation, 35–6
reported speech, 49–51
Reported Speech, 112–13, 126
role play, 32, 39–40, 59–60, 64–5,
   71, 79
Russian: address forms, 54; language
   items, 54

Sadrina Project, The, 43–5, 48, 127
SECAM, television system, 122
self-study, 11, 33
setting, 62, 64–5
silent sequences, 73–6, 76–7, 78,
   111–12
simple past: in English, 48; in
   German, 48
simple present in English, 52, 87–8,
   114
'shorties', 86–9
slang, 47
socio-linguistic rules, 45–7, 53–4,
   64–5, 110
software, 118–21
sound: recording with, 94, 97, 101–2;
   techniques for exploiting, 73–9; *see
   also* audio
soundtrack, 29, 77, 123–4
Spanish, address forms, 54
Speak Easy, 74, 88, 127
specific purposes, language for,
   16–17, 23–4, 24–6, 28, 35–6, 42,
   43–5, 45–6, 48, 59, 73, 114,
   126–7
speculation, 51–3
stereo soundtrack, 77, 123
Switch On, 29, 74–5, 127
Systems One, 73, 127